ZOMBIES HATE STUFF

GREG STONES

CHRONICLE BOOKS

SAN FRANCISCO

LIBRARY OF CONGRESS CATALOGING-IN-PUBLICATION DATA
Stones, Greg.
Zombies hate stuff / Greg Stones.
    p. cm.
ISBN 978-1-4521-0740-0
1. Zombies—Humor I. Title.
PN6231.Z6S76 2012
791.43'675—dc23

                          2011026086

Manufactured in China
Designed by Michael Morris

10 9 8 7 6

Chronicle Books LLC
680 Second Street
San Francisco, California 94107
www.chroniclebooks.com

Chronicle Books publishes distinctive books and gifts. From award-
winning children's titles, best-selling cookbooks, and eclectic pop
culture to acclaimed works of art and design, stationery, and
journals, we craft publishing that's instantly recognizable for its
spirit and creativity. Enjoy our publishing and become part of our
community at www.chroniclebooks.com.

ZOMBIES

HATE . . .

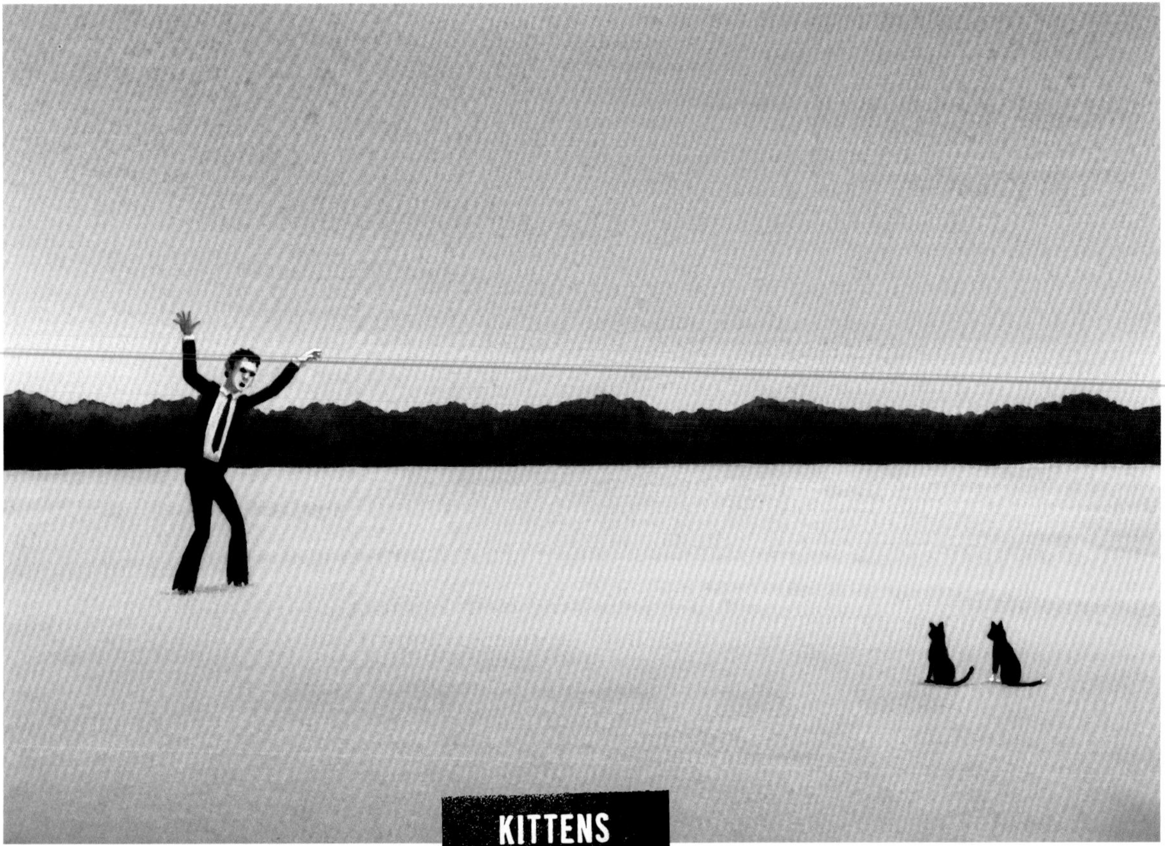

KITTENS

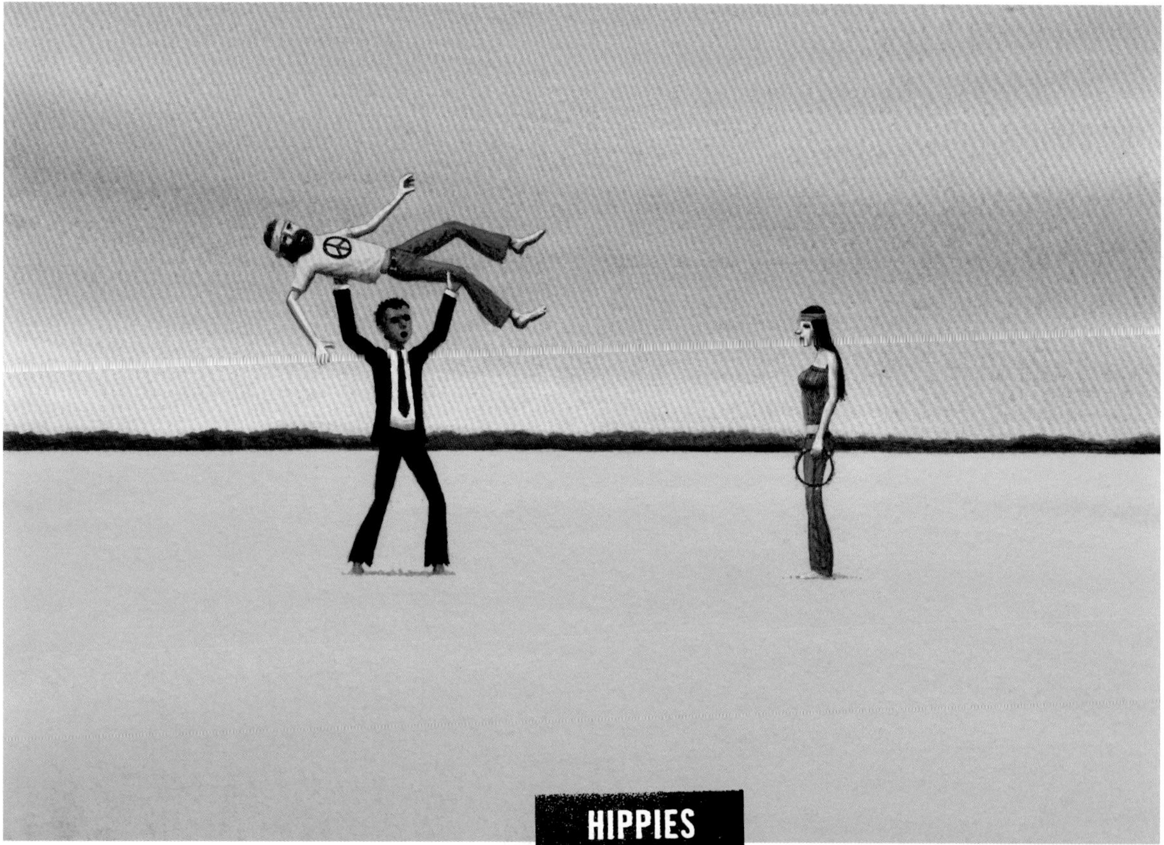

HIPPIES

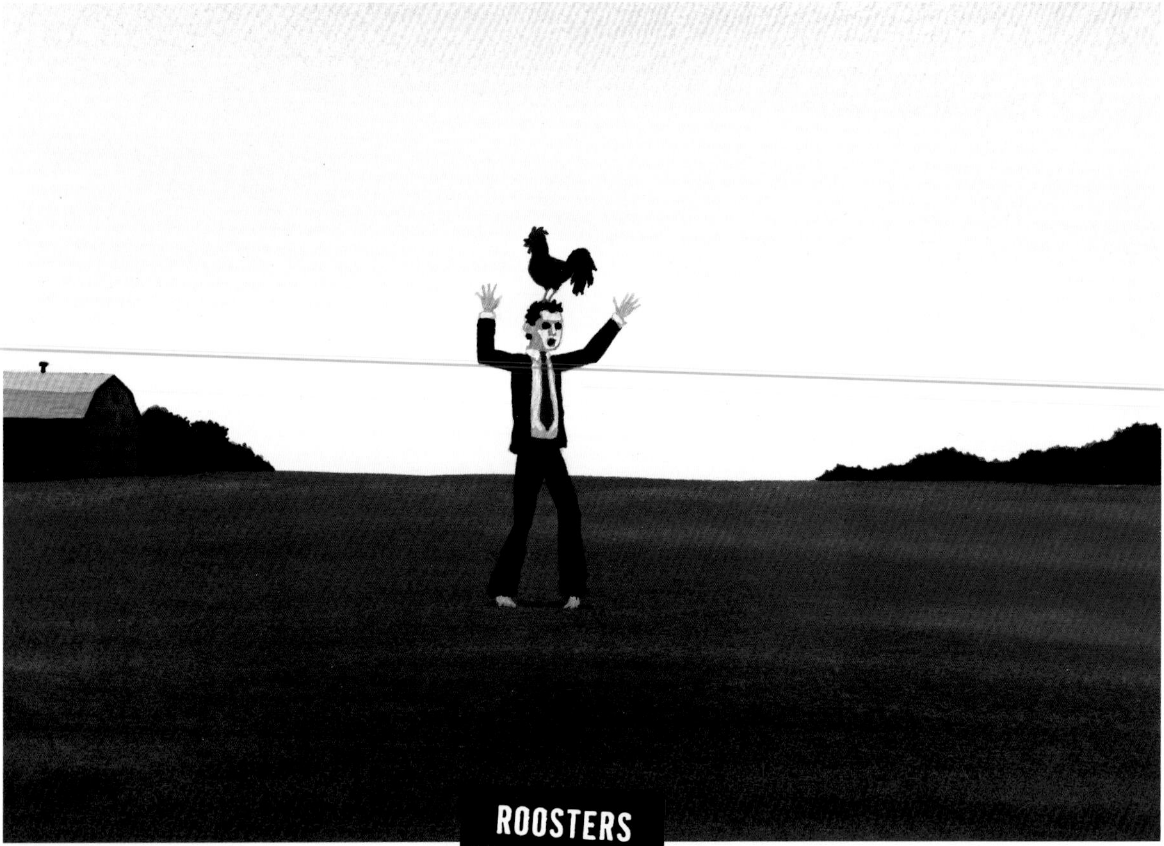

ROOSTERS

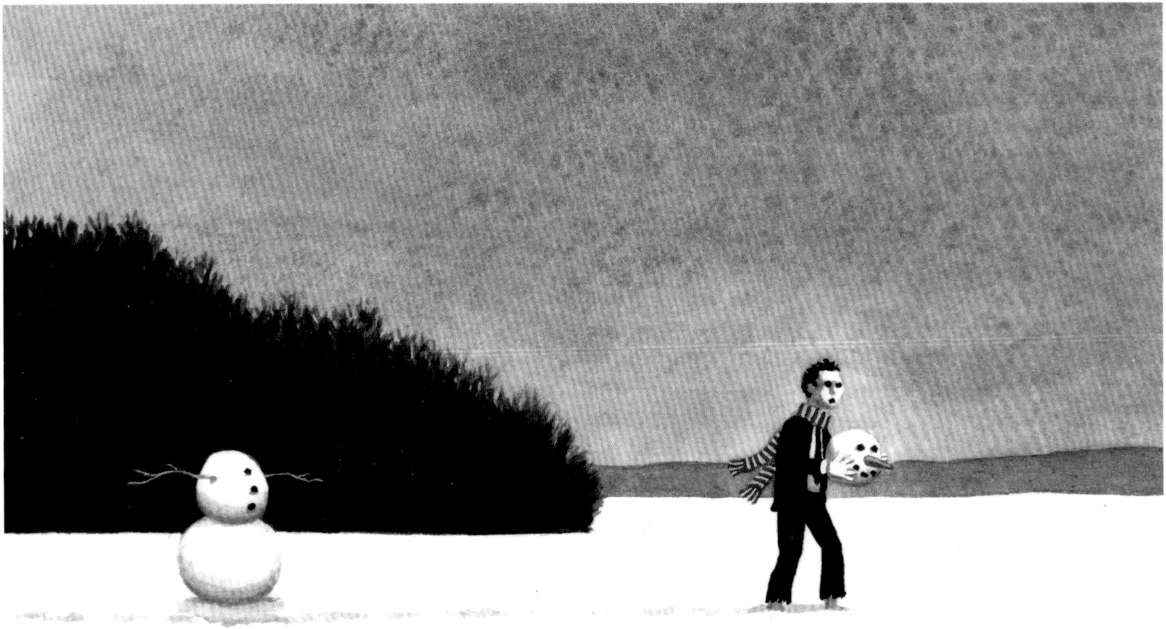

SNOWMEN

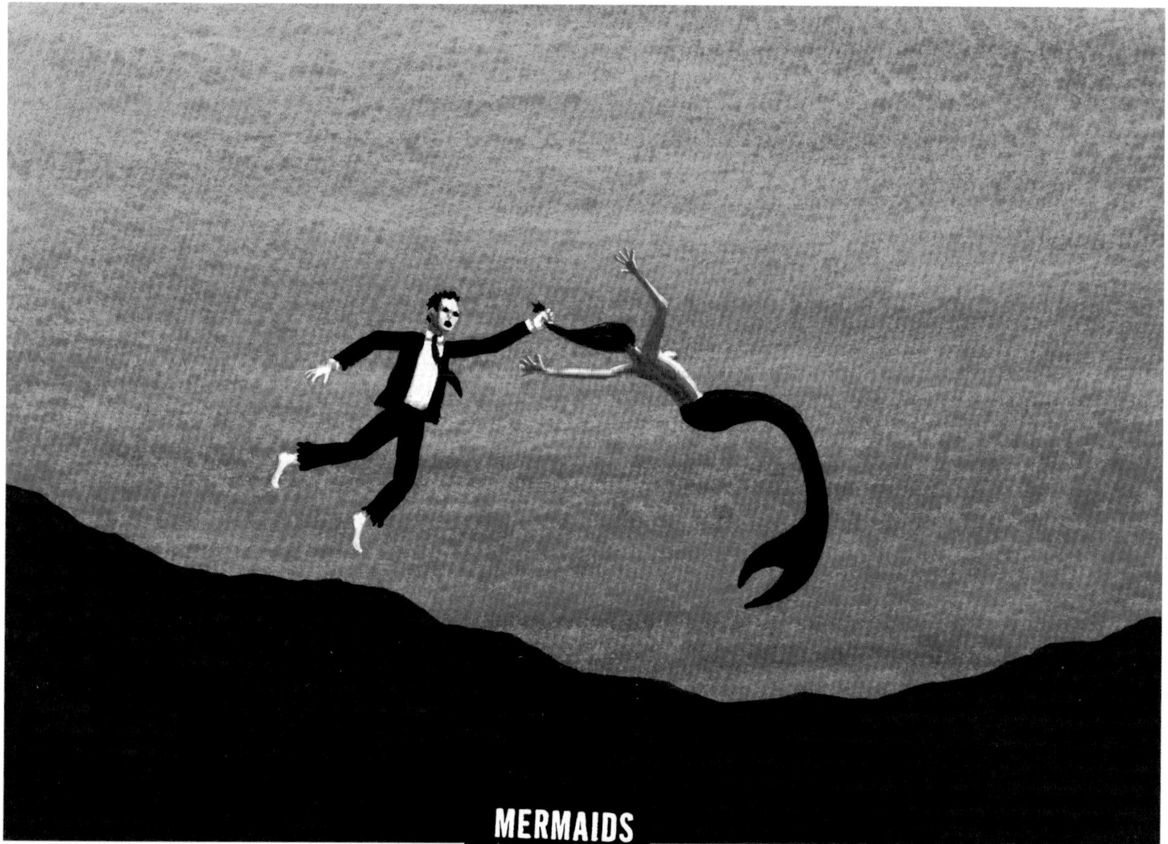

MERMAIDS

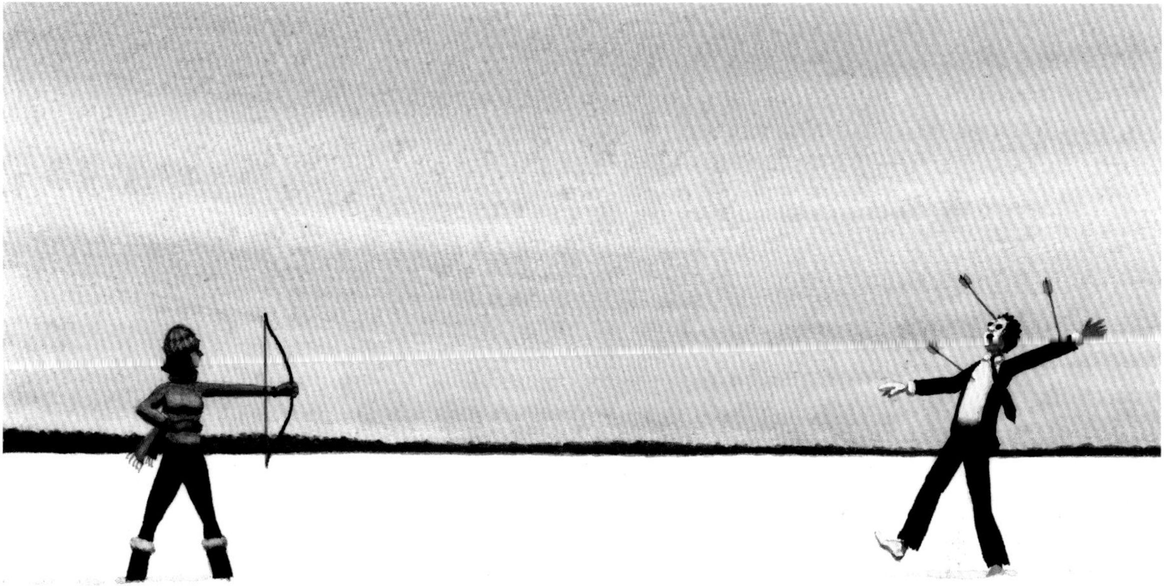

ARCHERY

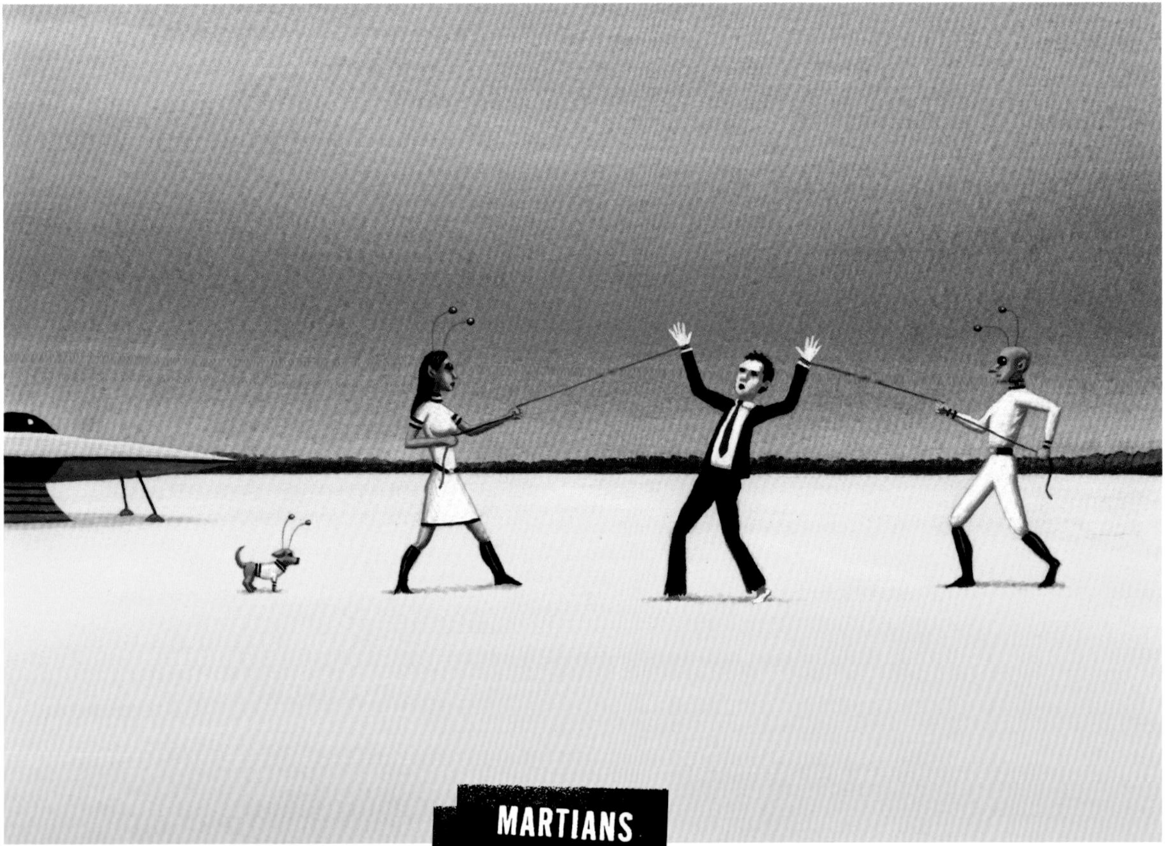

MARTIANS

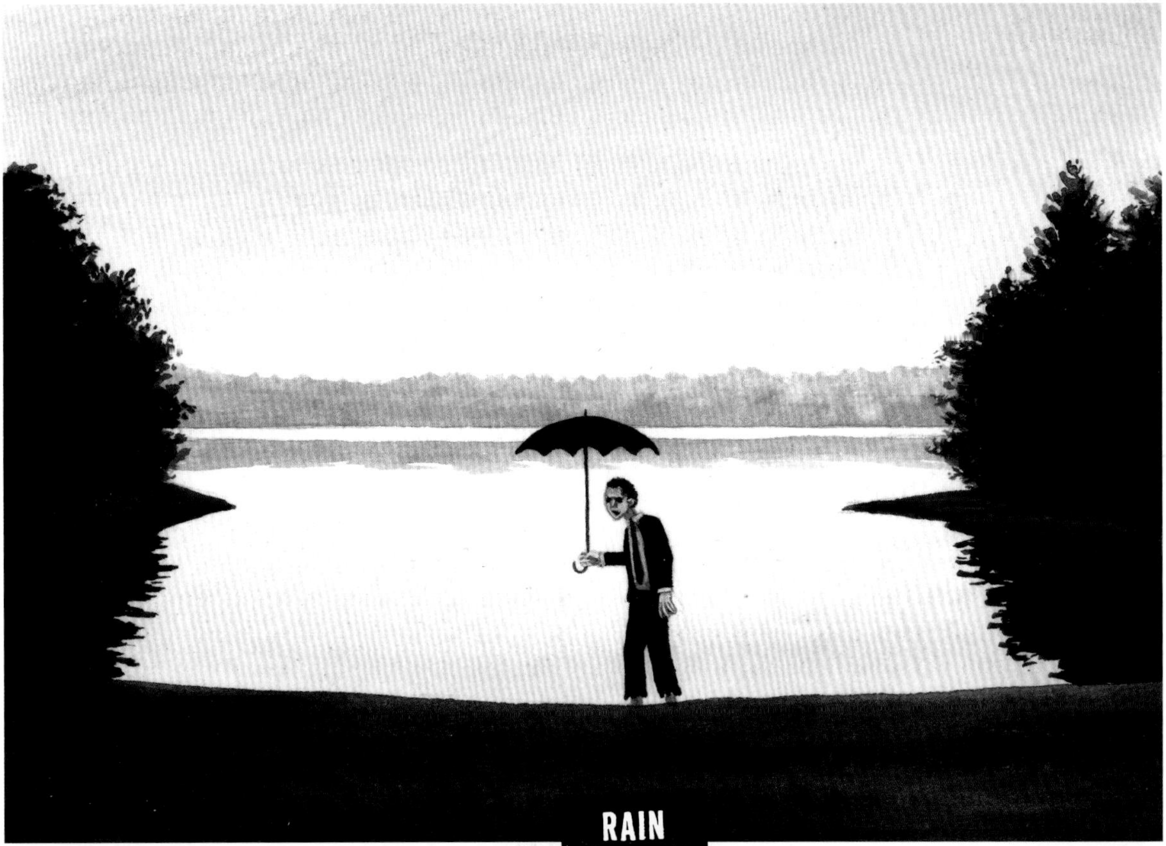

RAIN

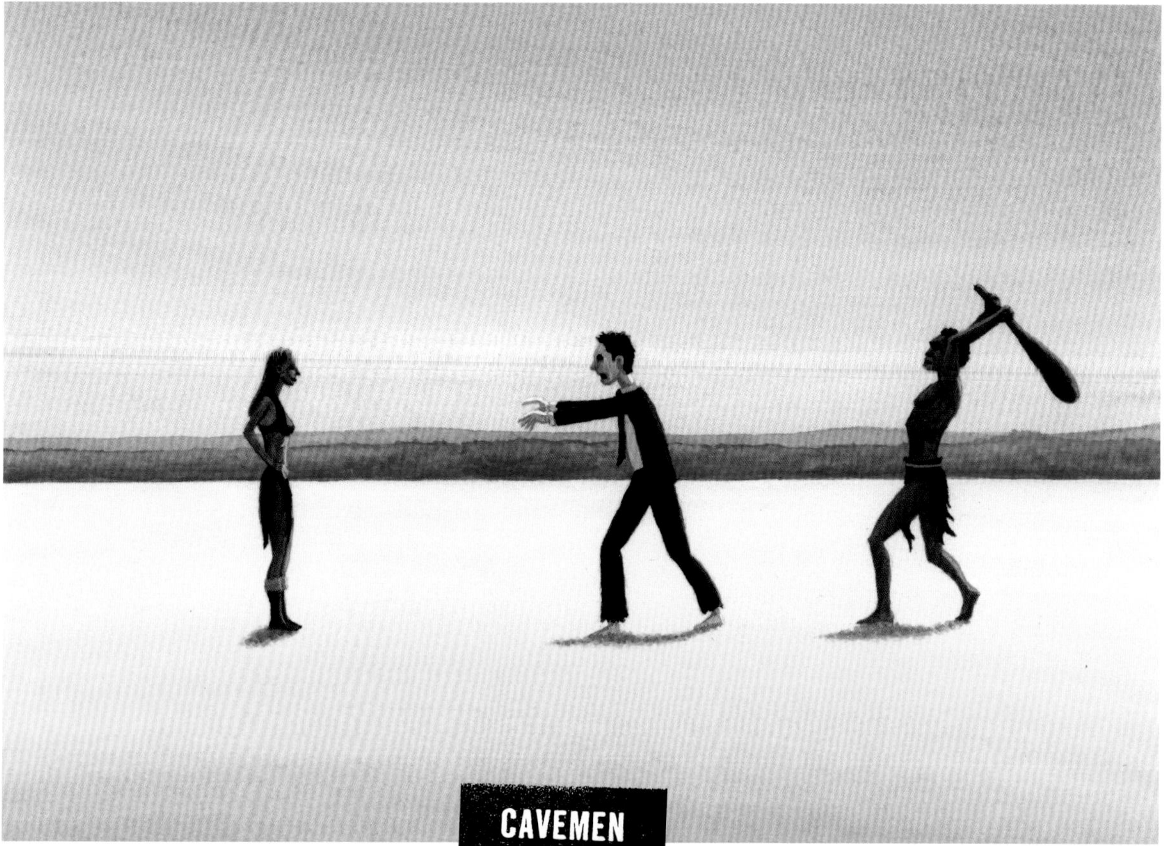

CAVEMEN

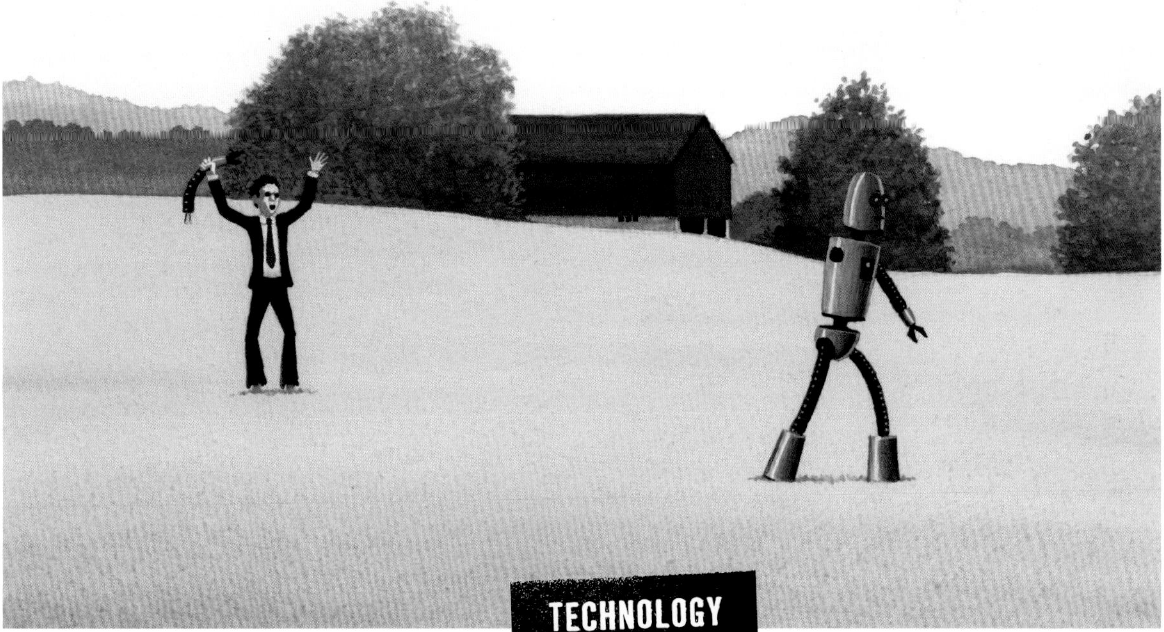

TECHNOLOGY

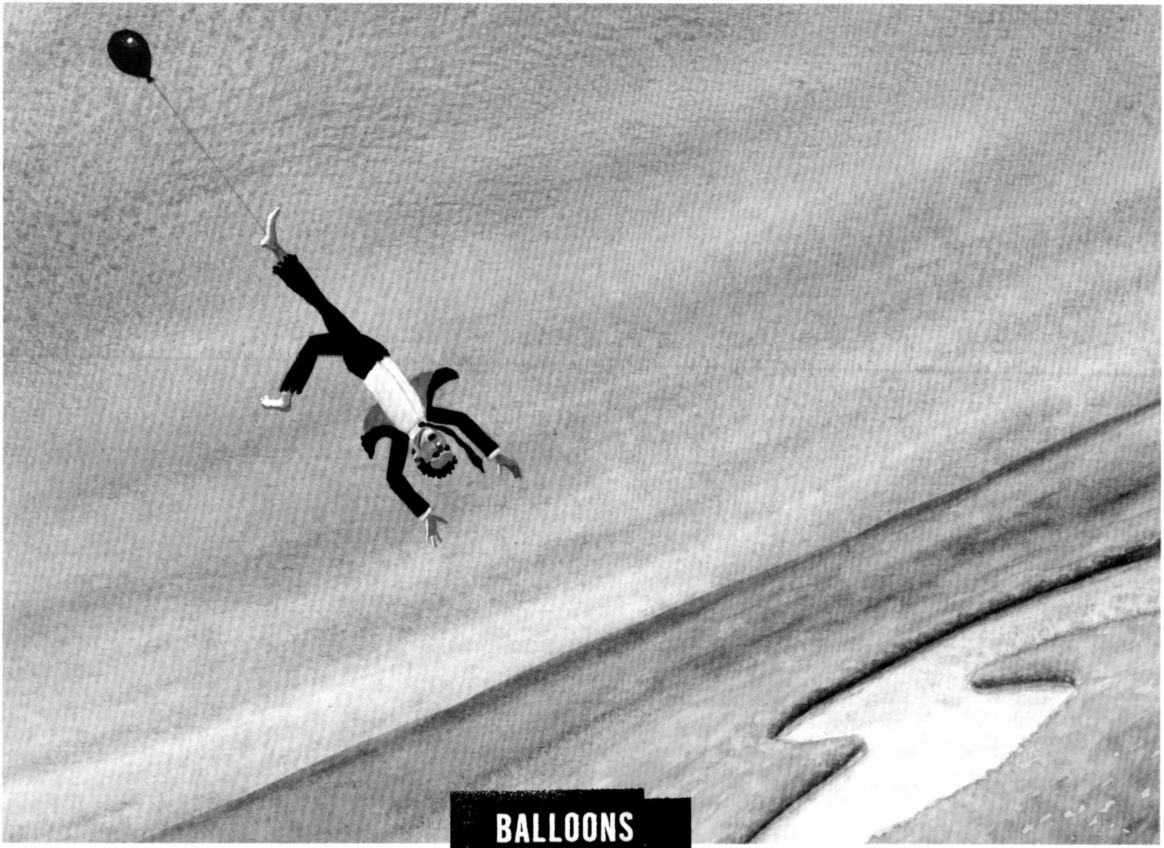

BALLOONS

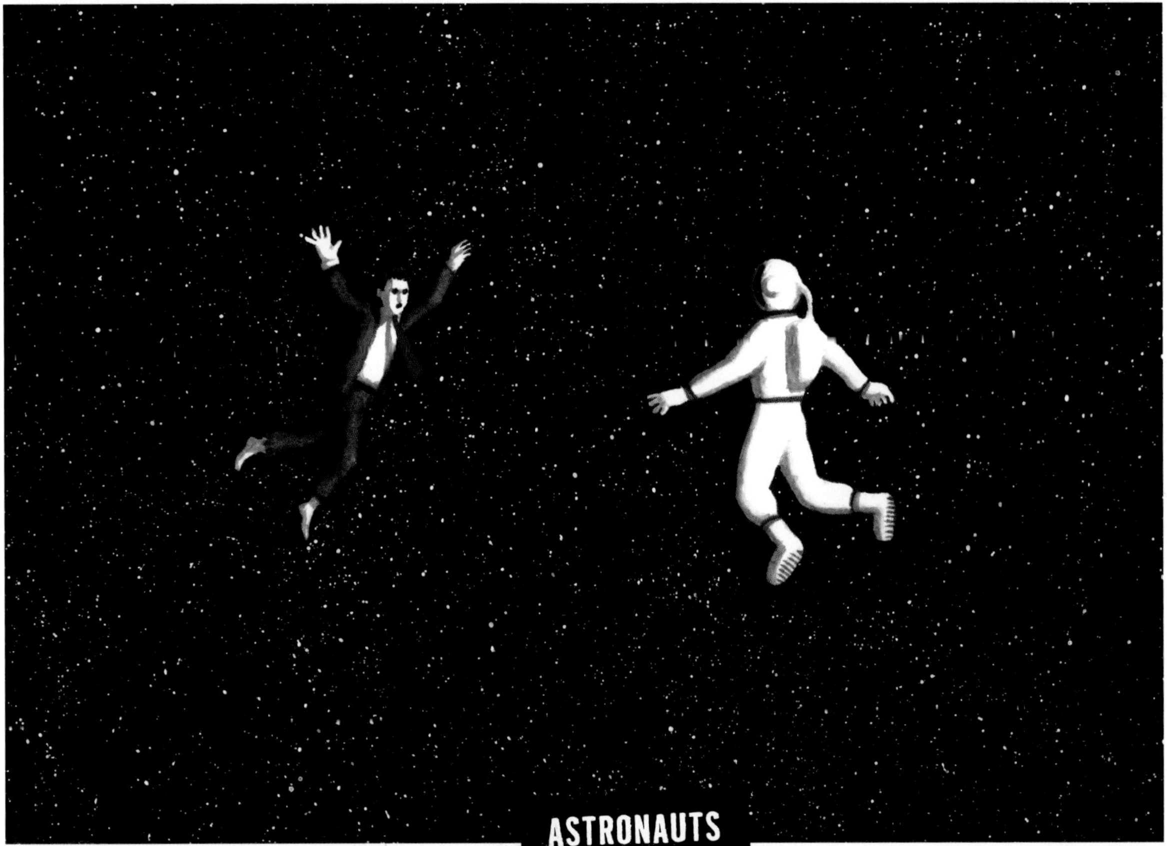

ASTRONAUTS

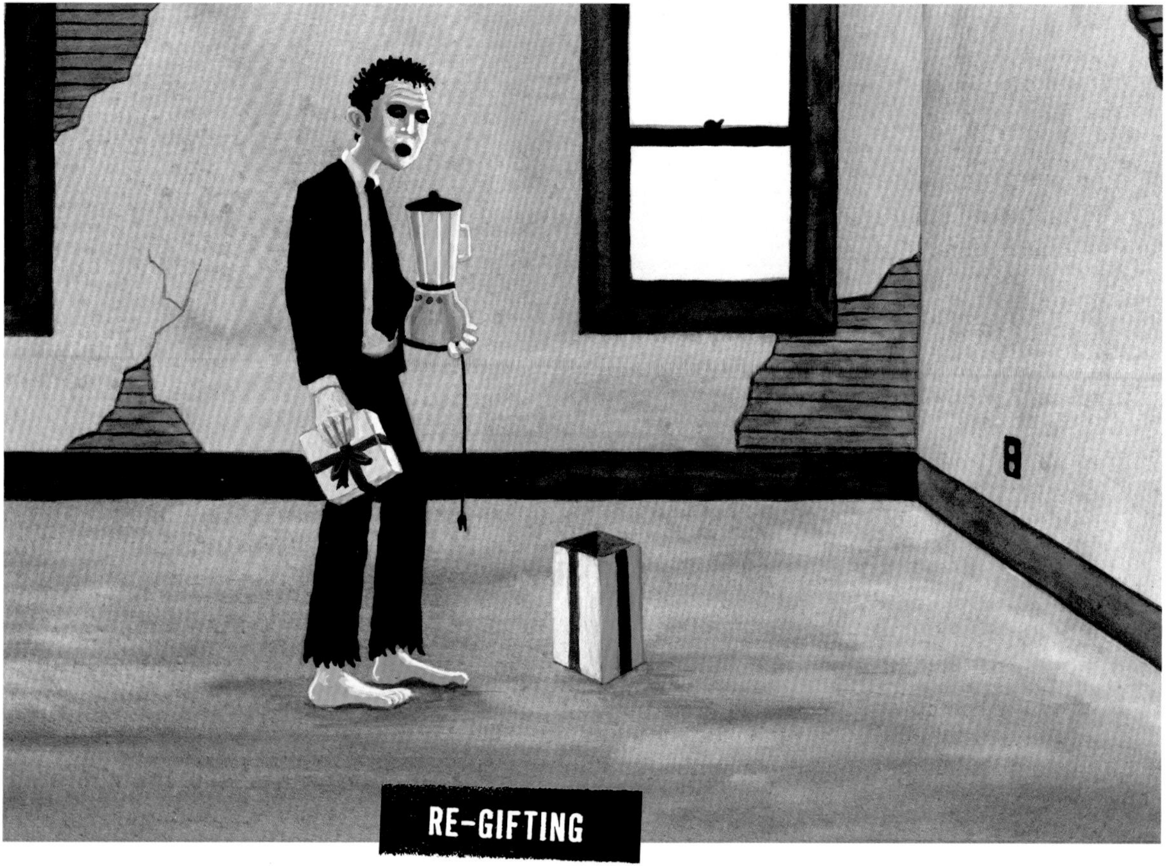

RE-GIFTING

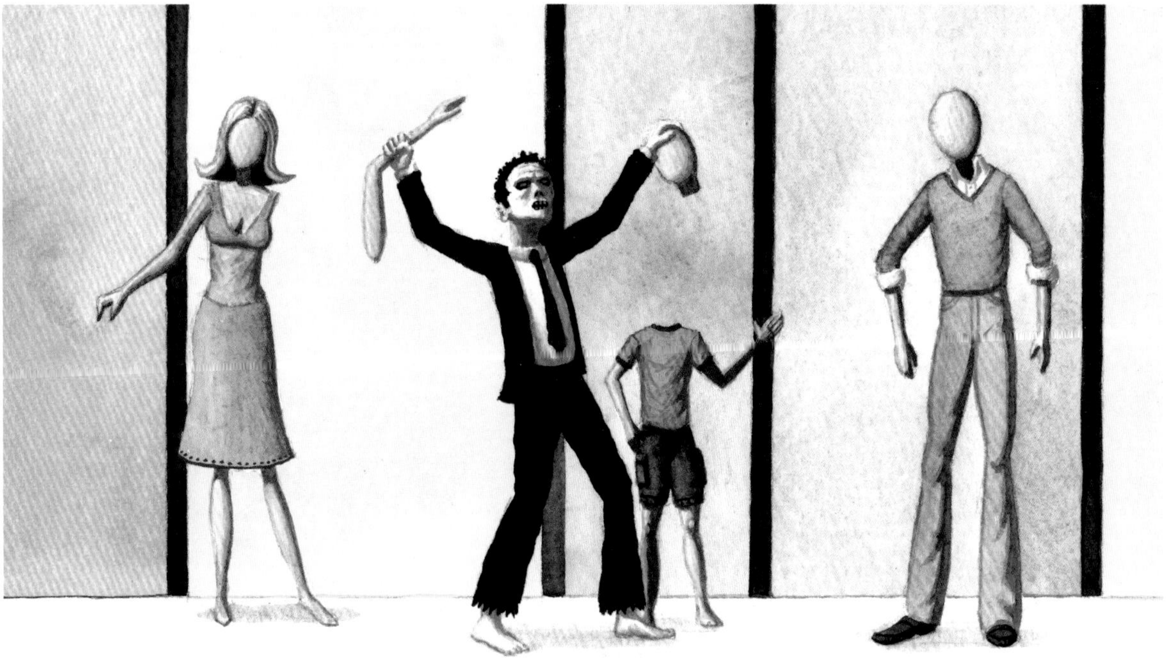

MANNEQUINS

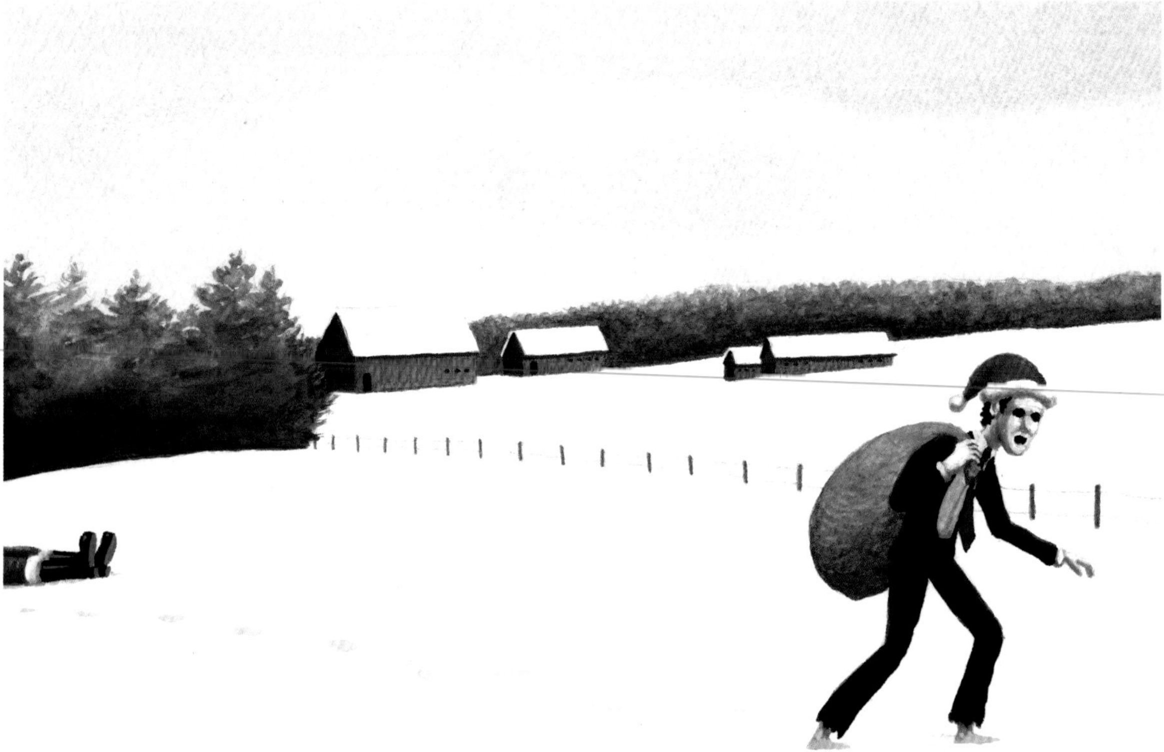

SANTA

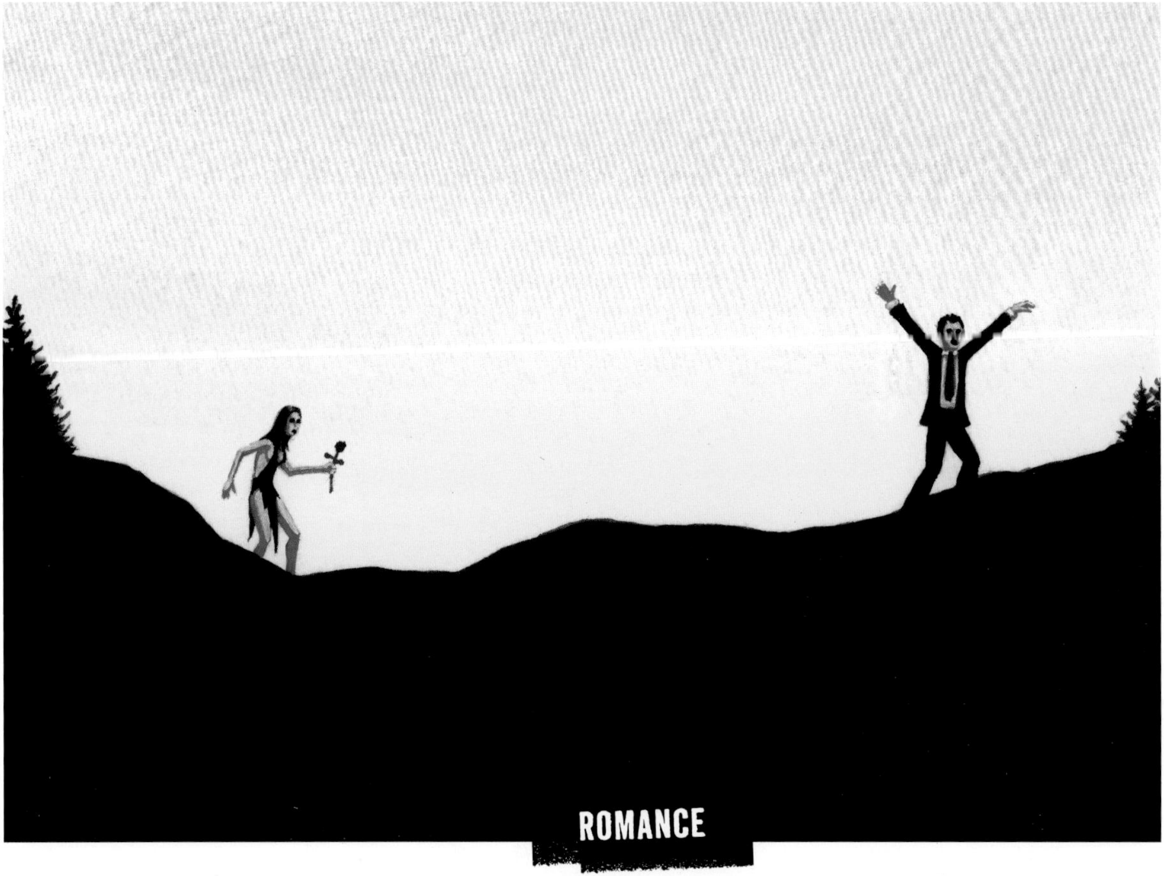

ROMANCE

SHEEP

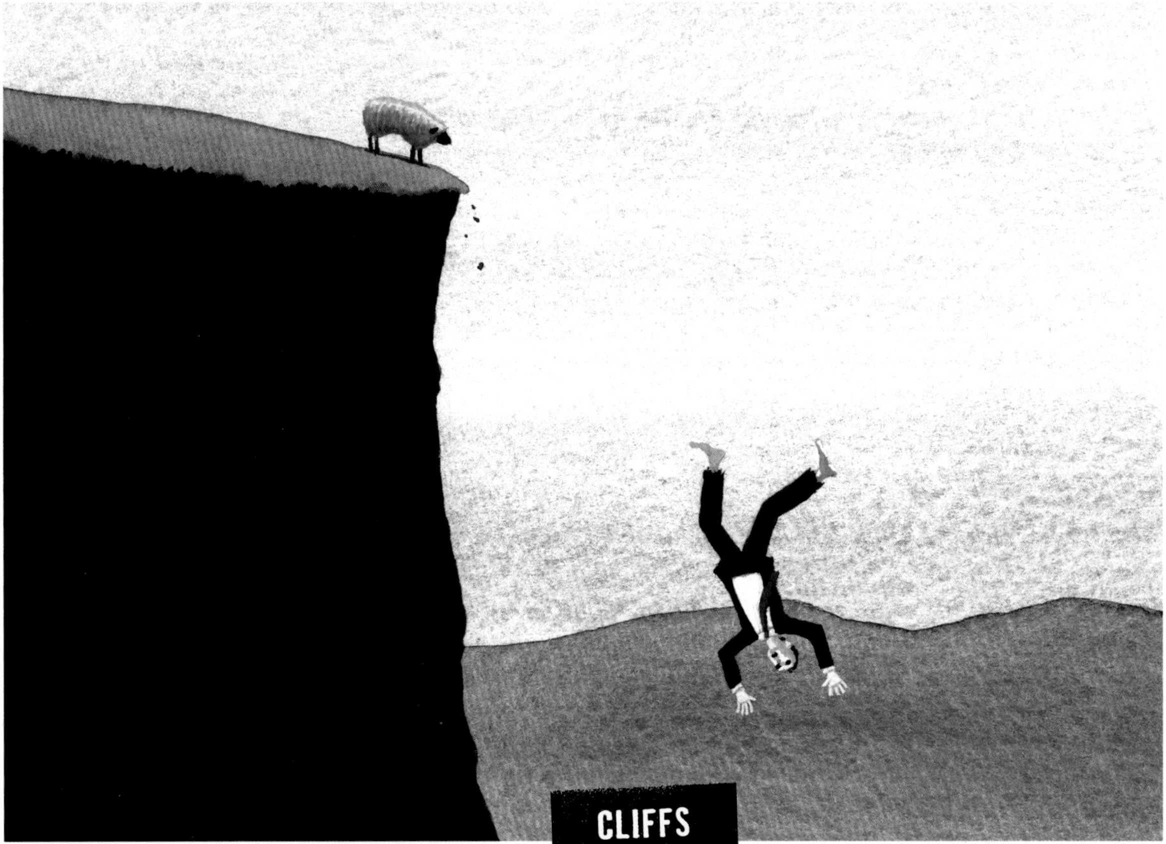

CLIFFS

WEDDINGS

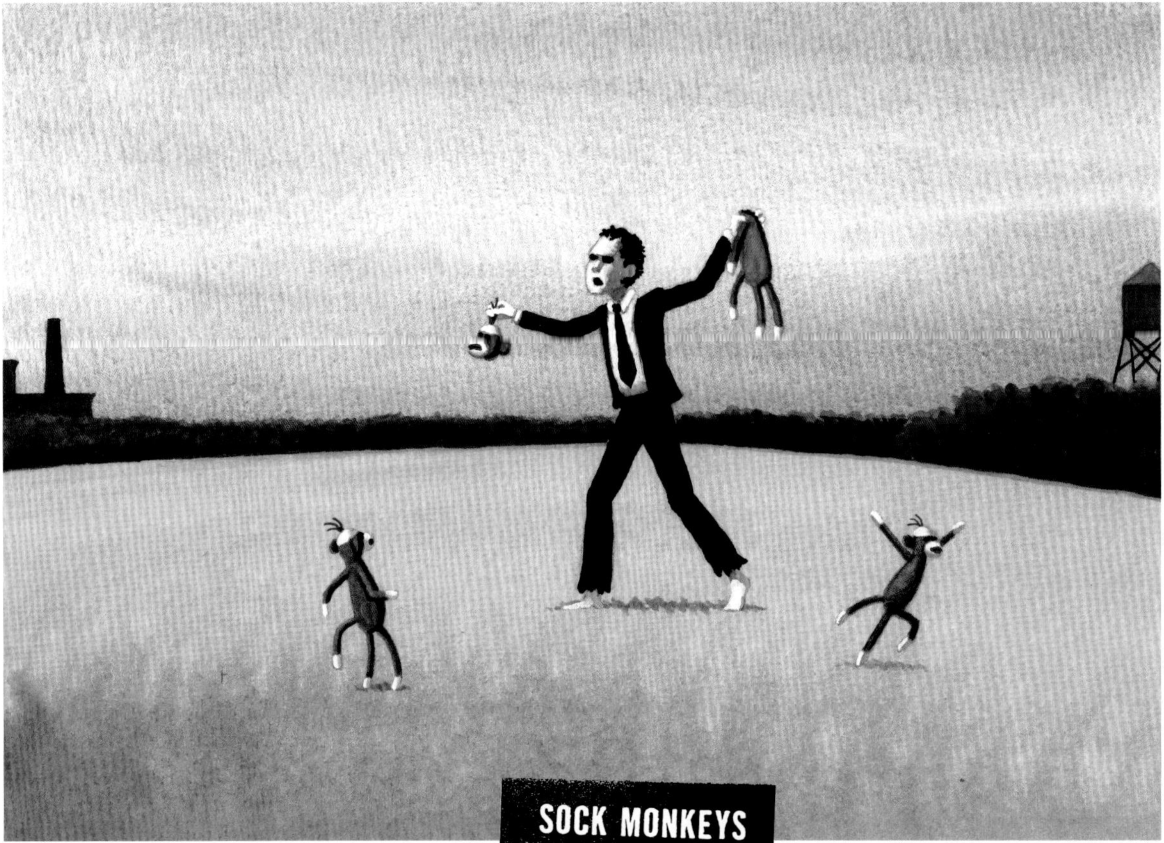

SOCK MONKEYS

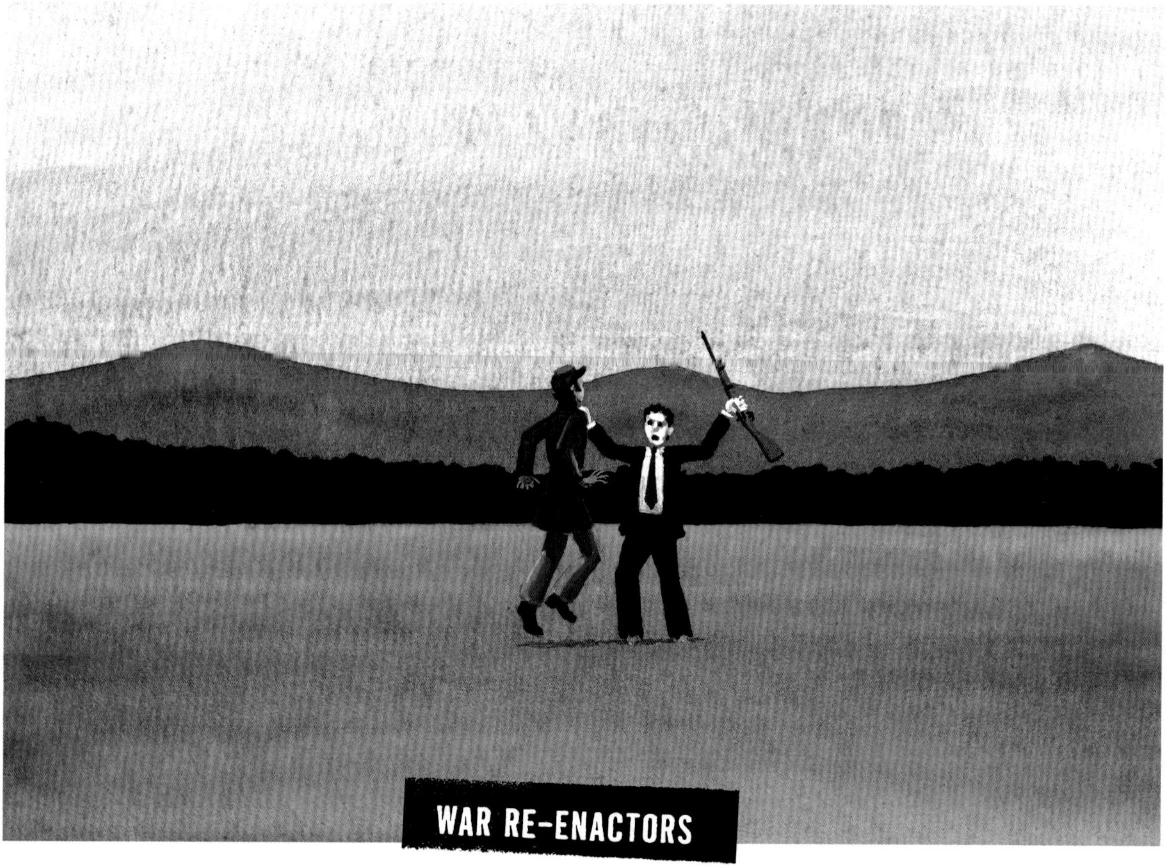
WAR RE-ENACTORS

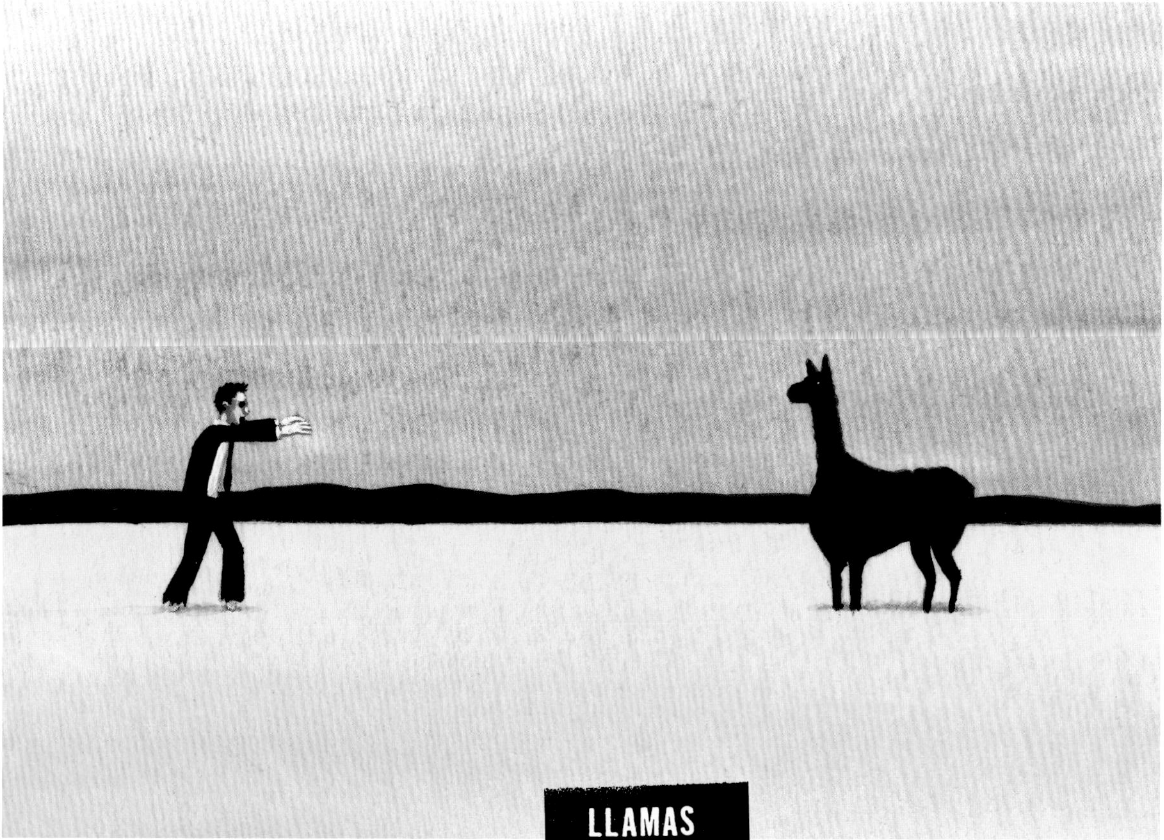

LLAMAS

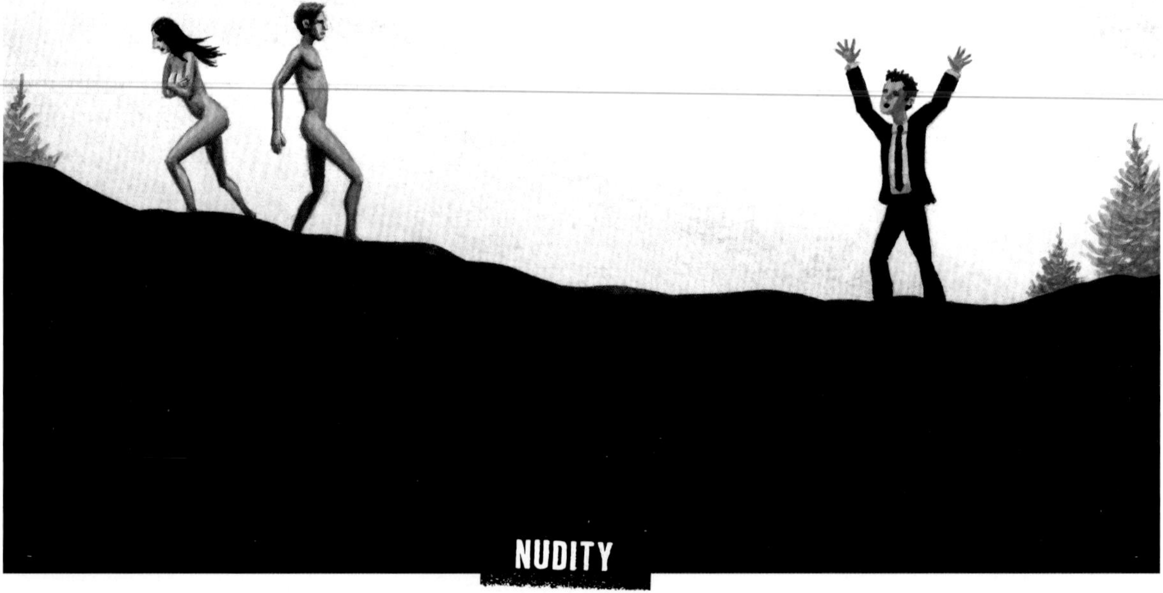
NUDITY

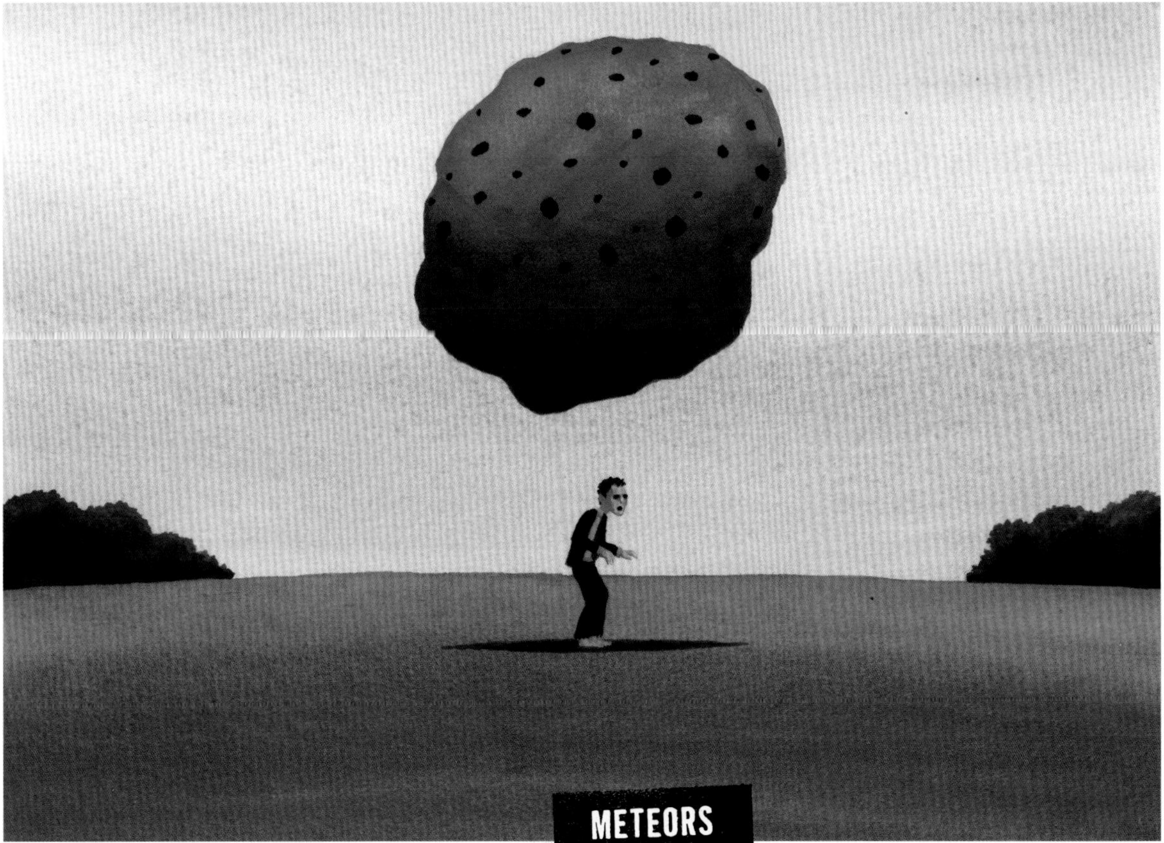

METEORS

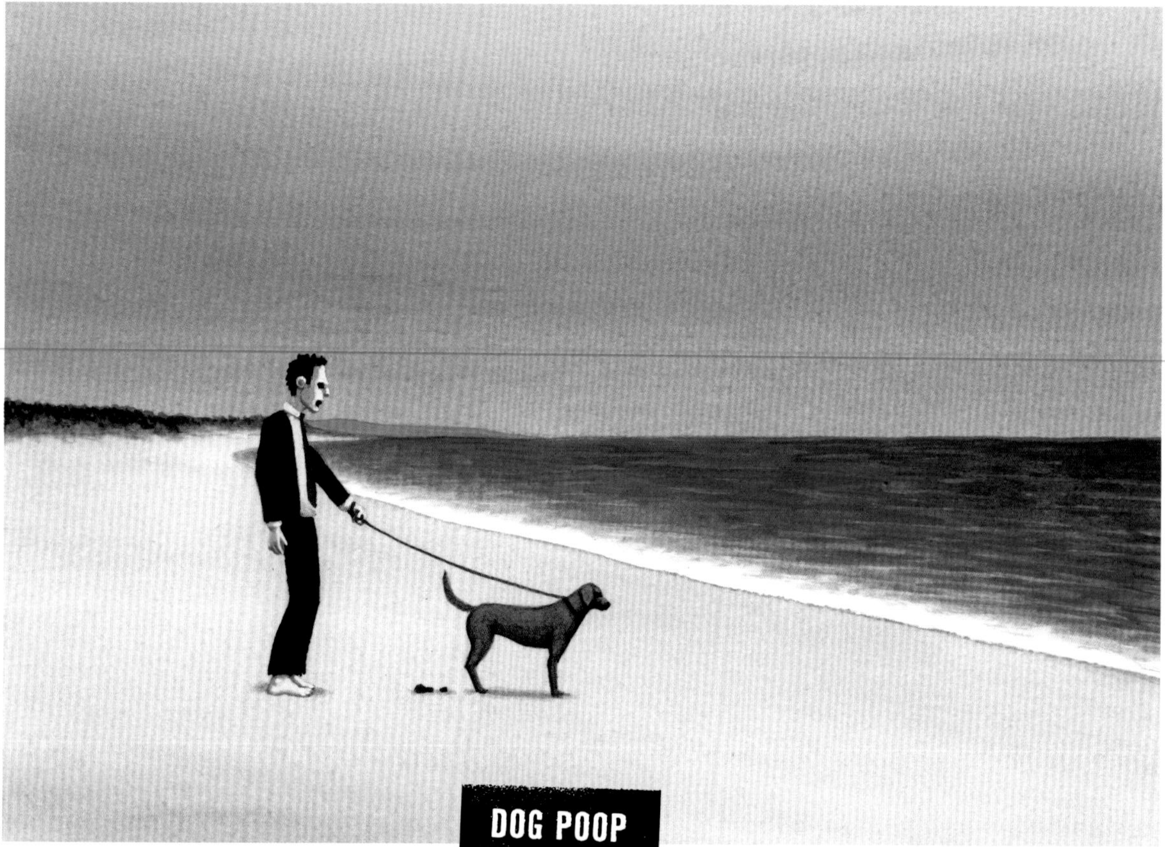

DOG POOP

ZOMBIES
DON'T MIND . . .

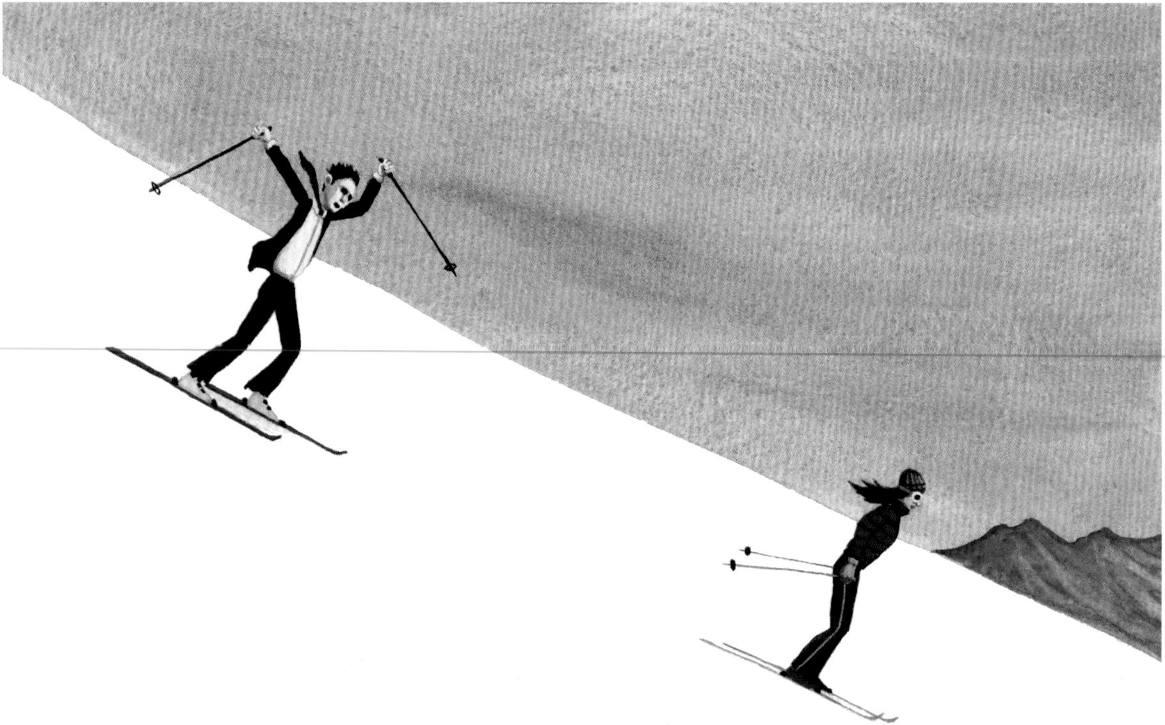

SKIING

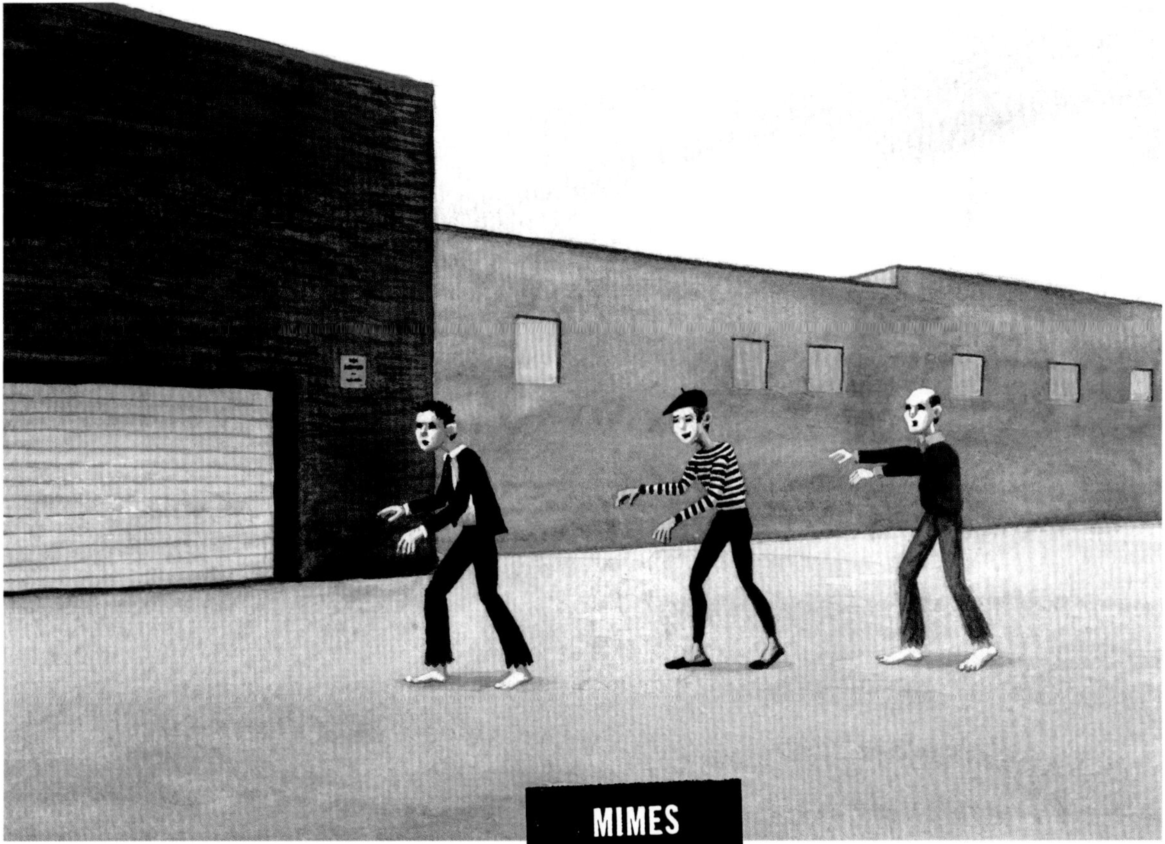

MIMES

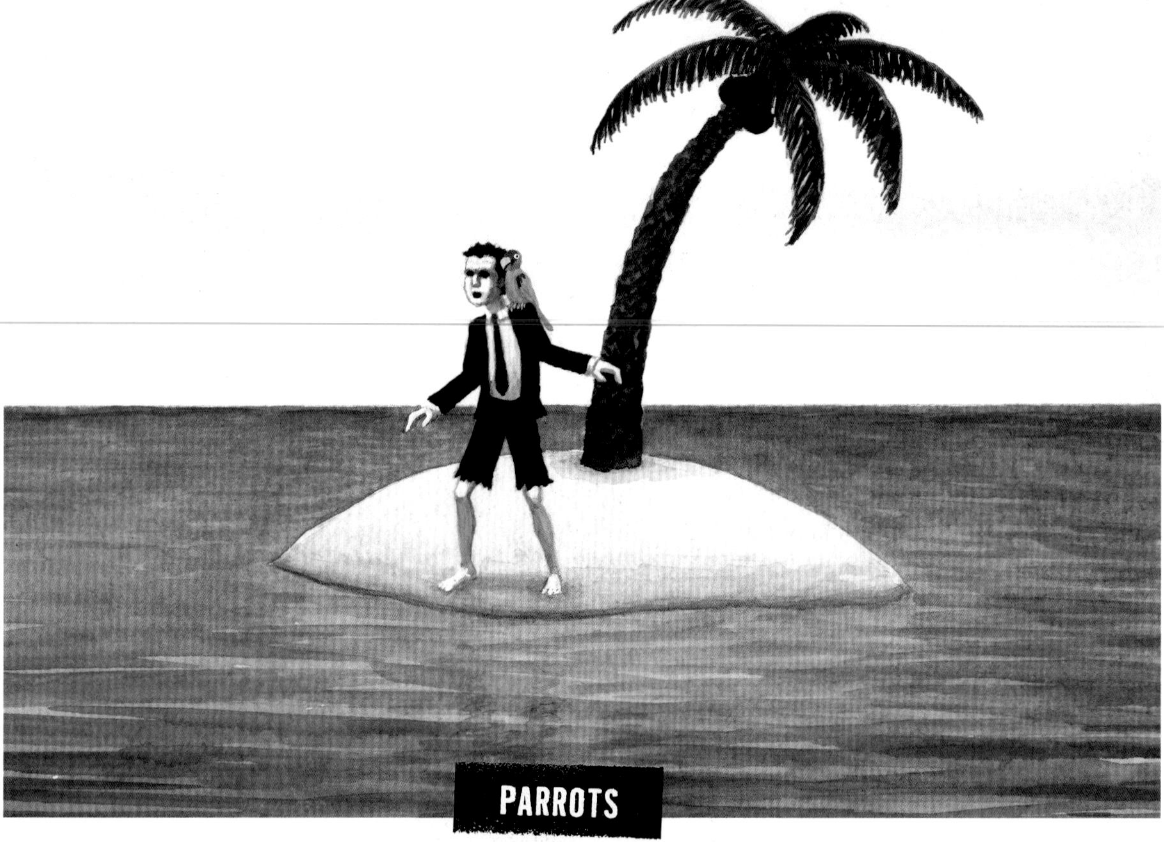
PARROTS

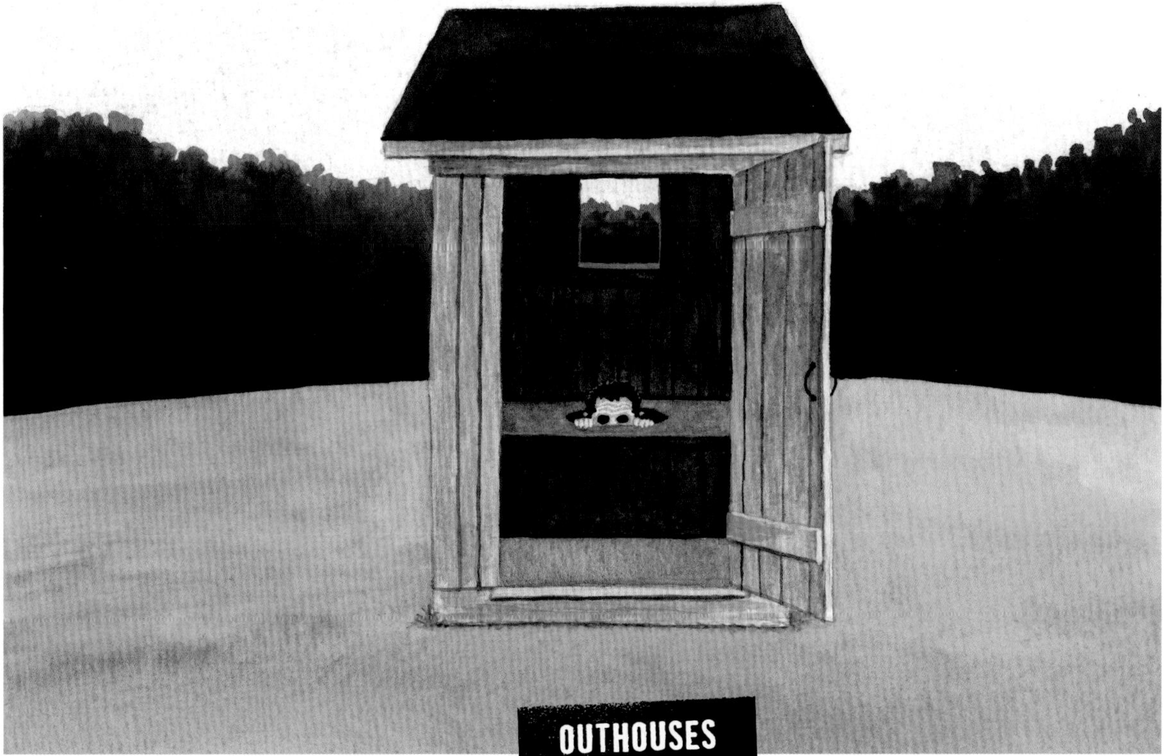

OUTHOUSES

CELERY

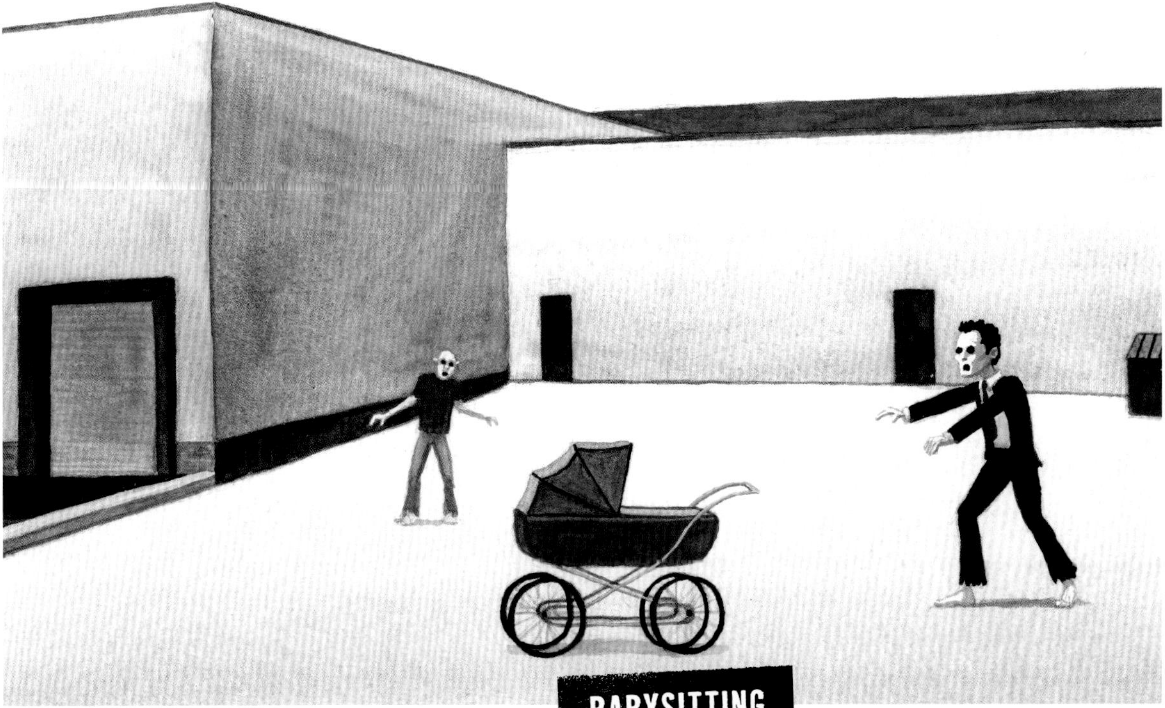

BABYSITTING

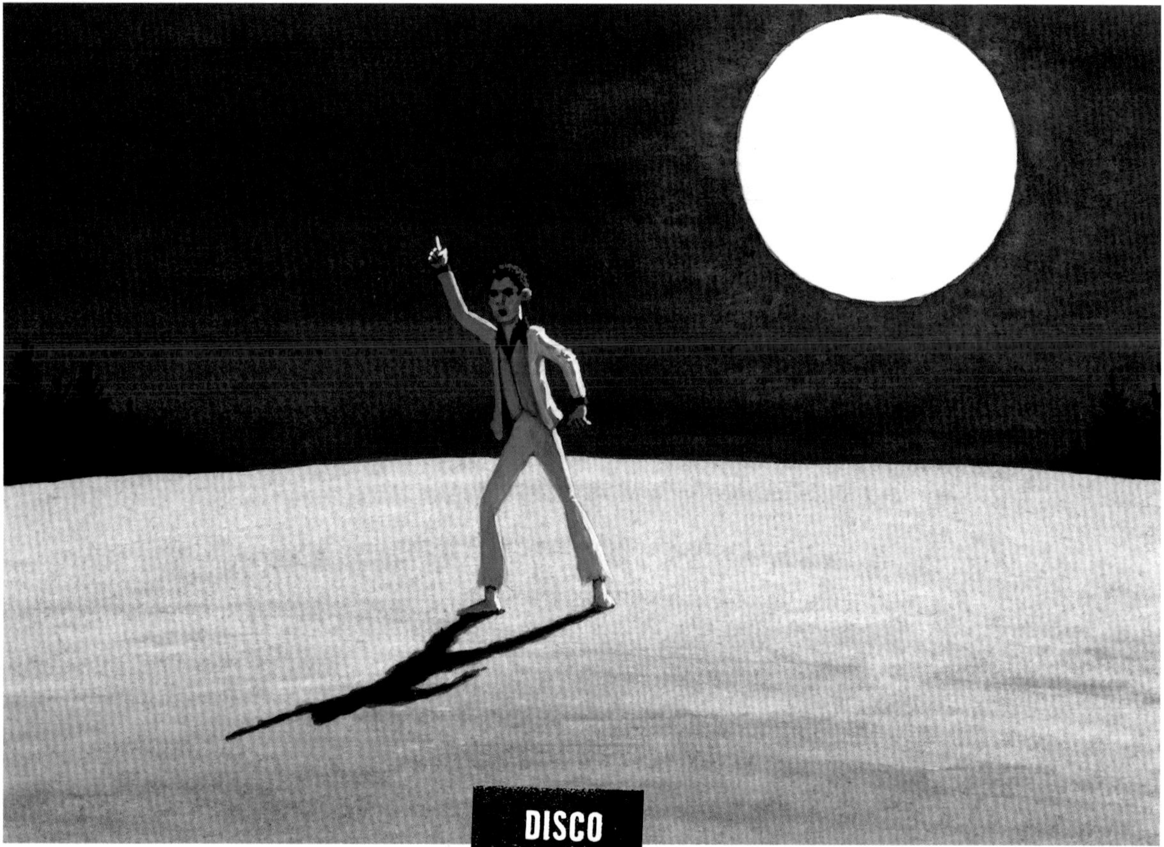

DISCO

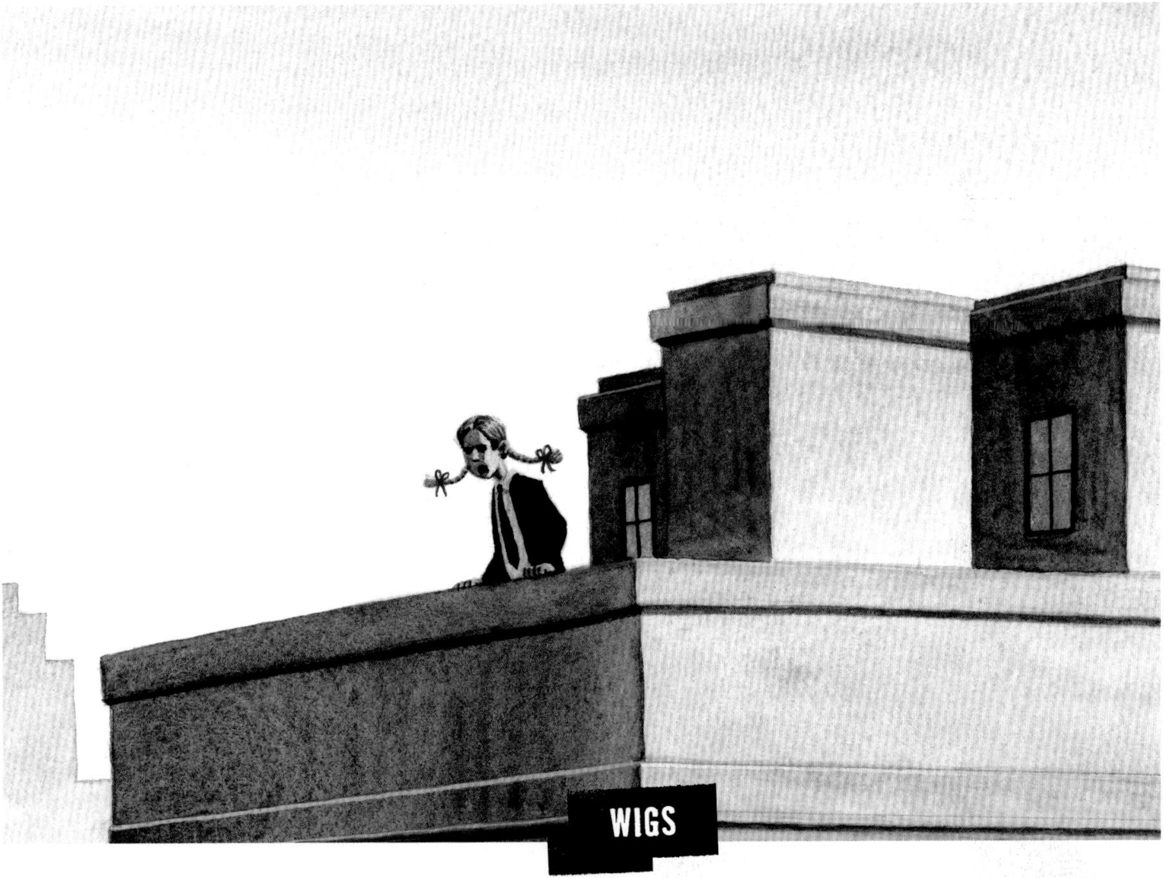
WIGS

CANADIANS

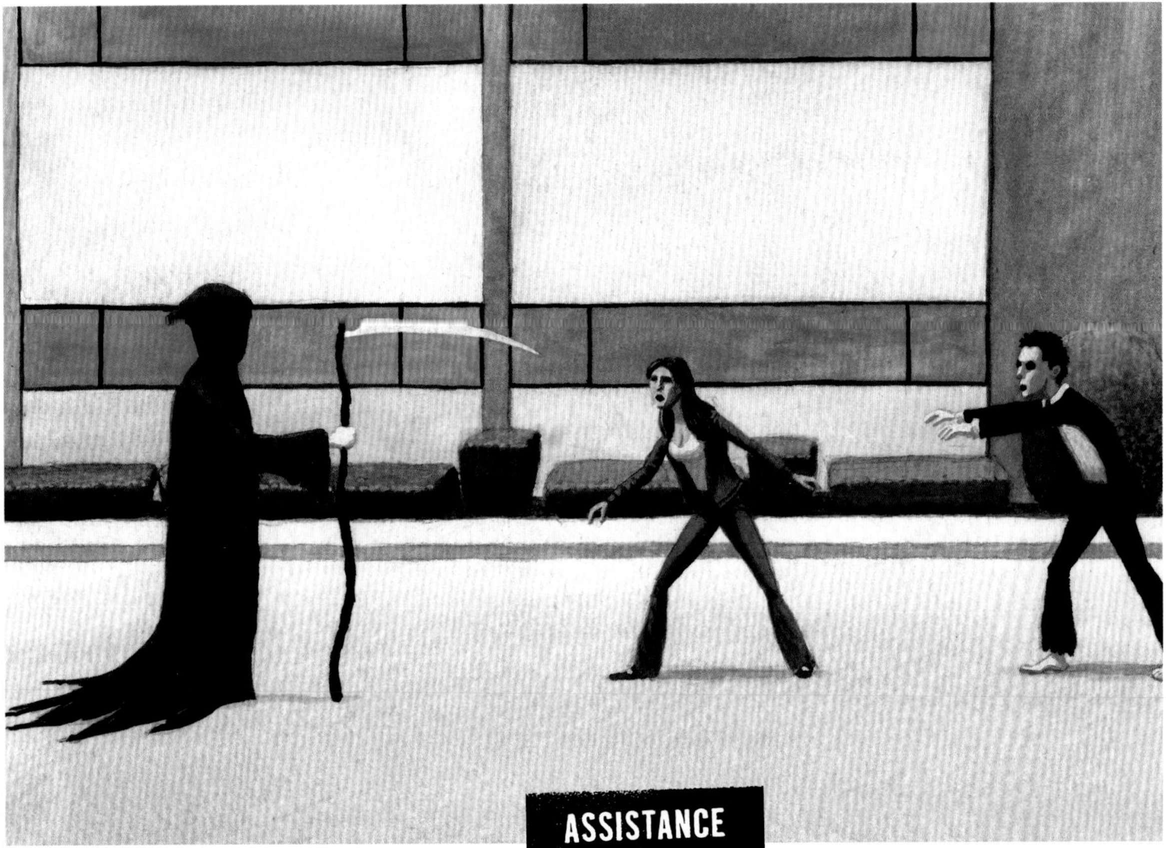

ASSISTANCE

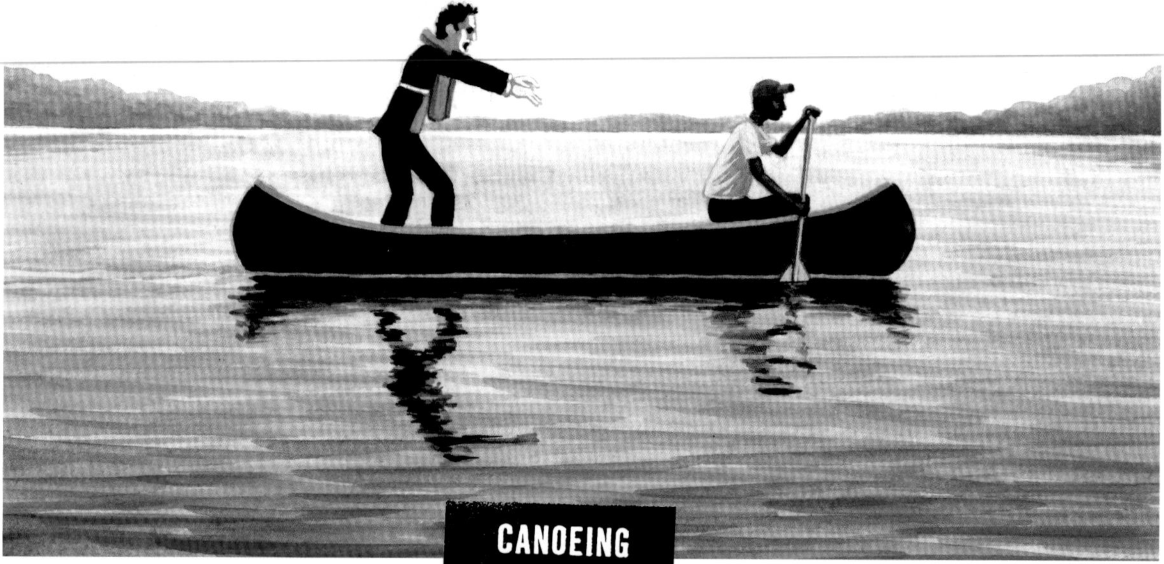

CANOEING

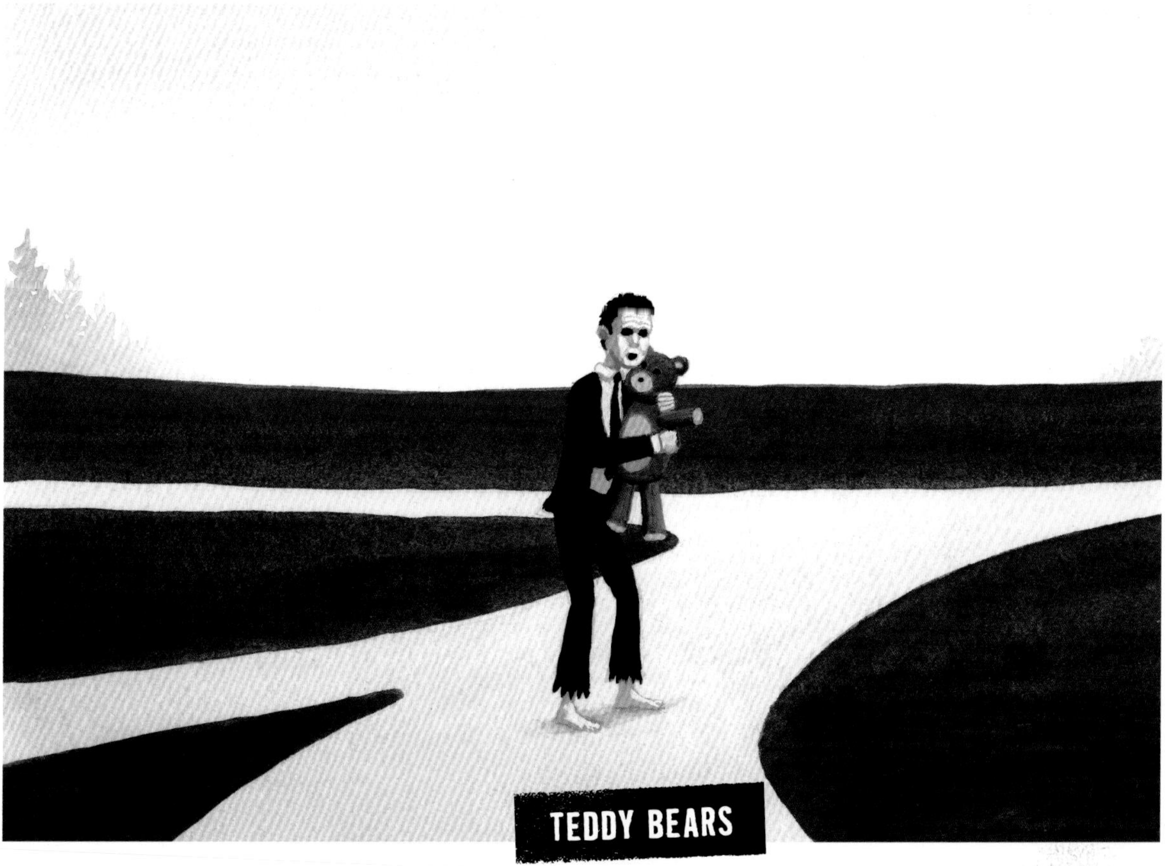

TEDDY BEARS

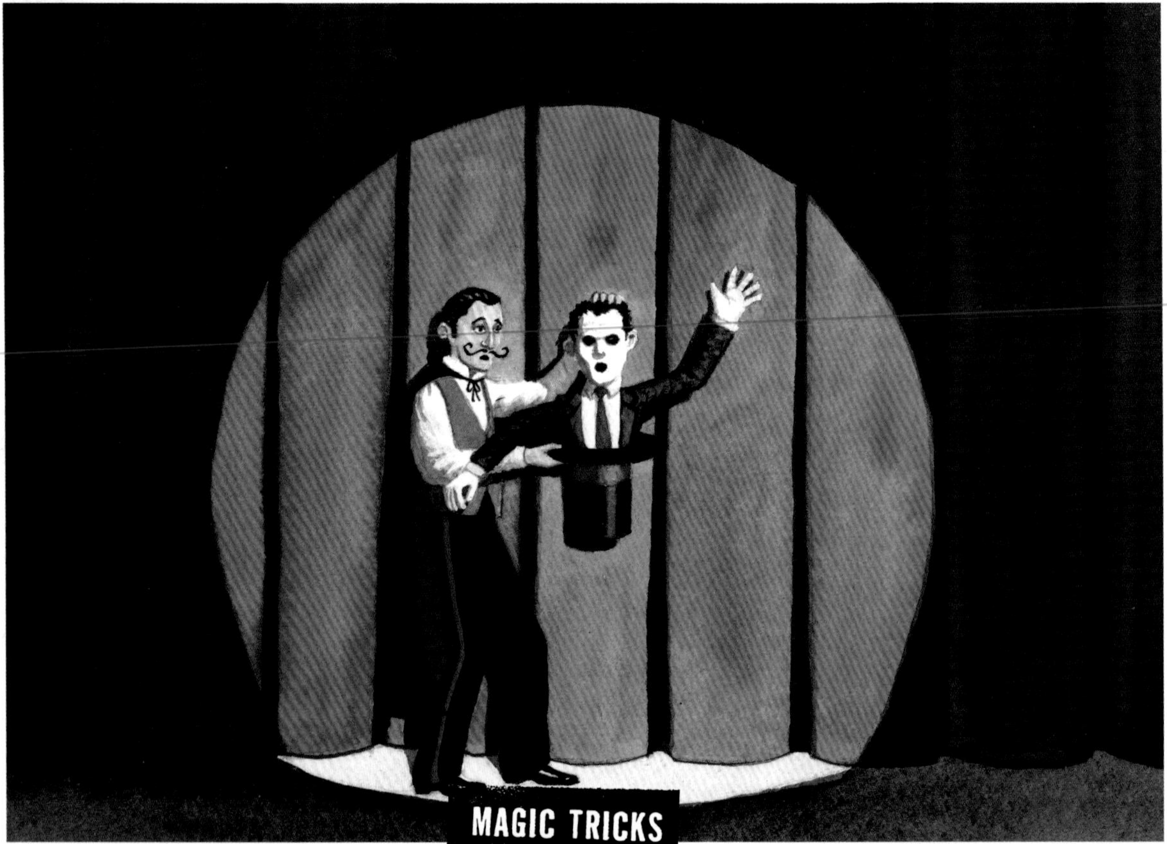

MAGIC TRICKS

ZOMBIES
REALLY HATE . . .

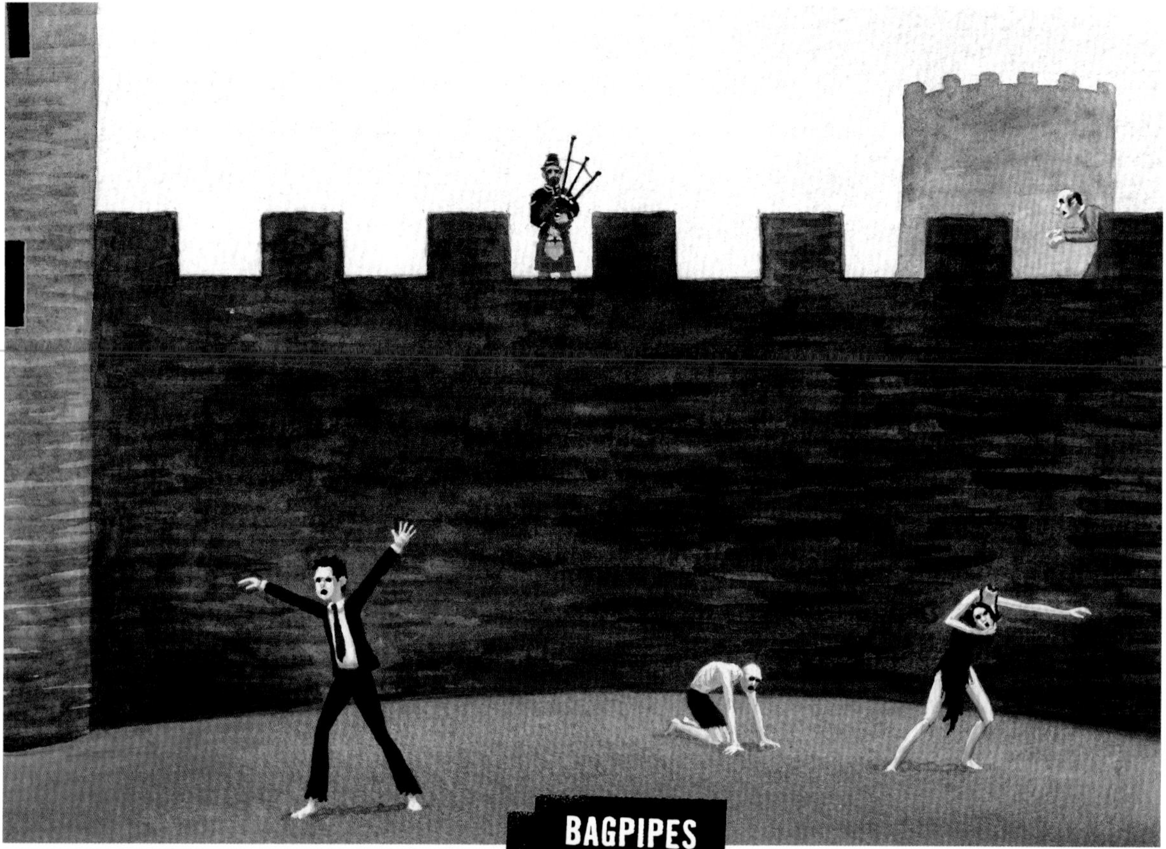

BAGPIPES

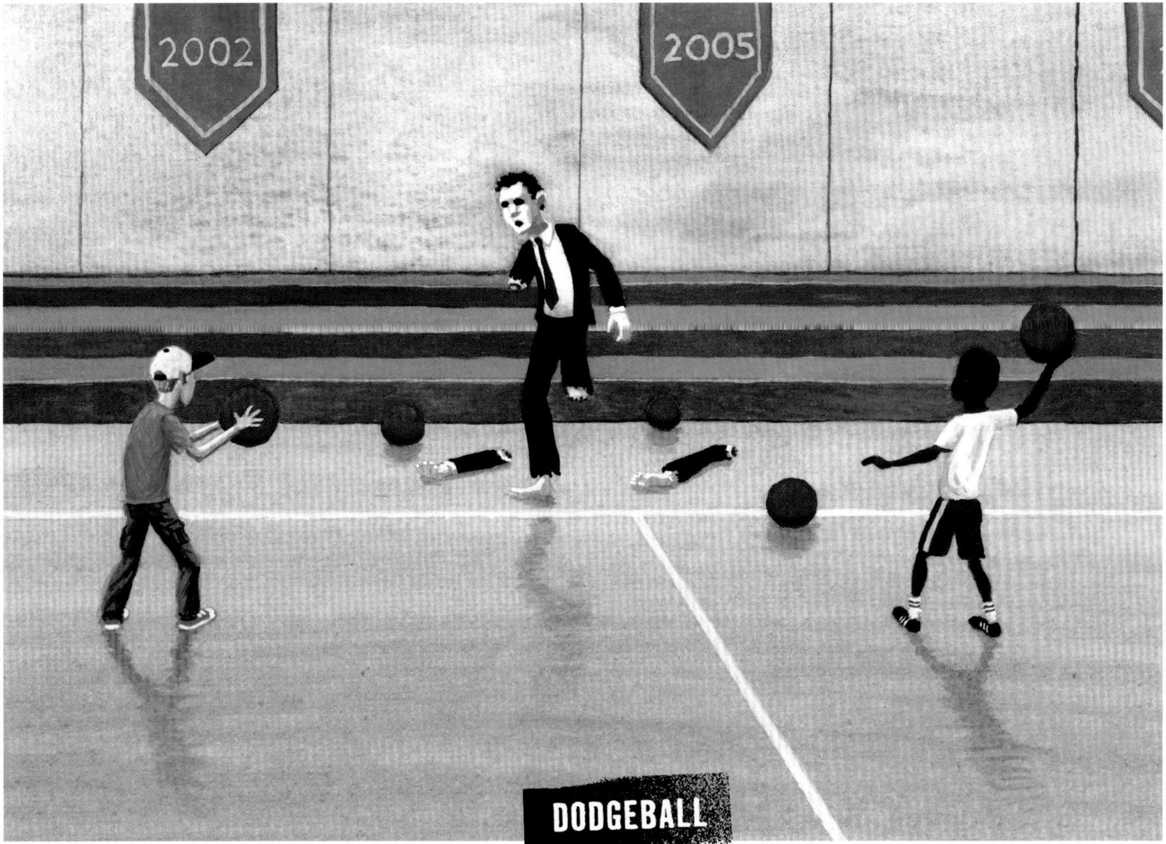
2002
2005

DODGEBALL

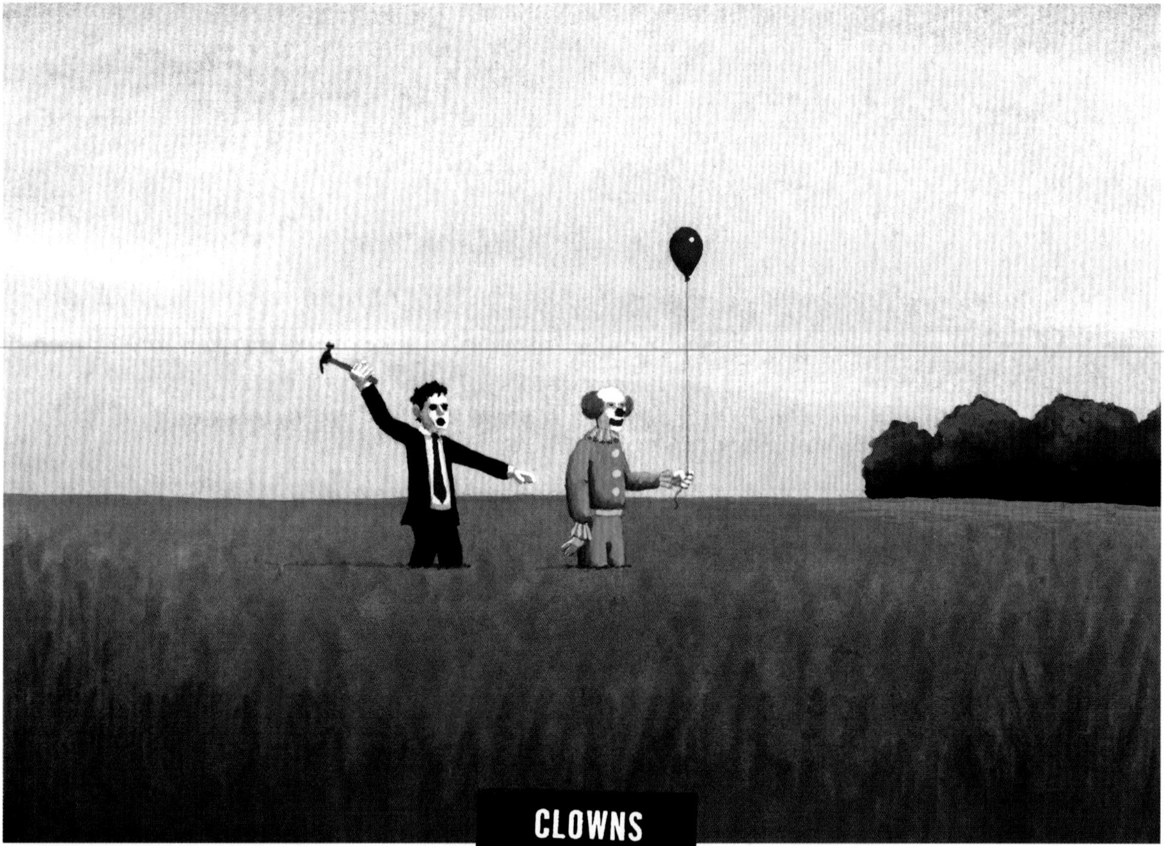

CLOWNS

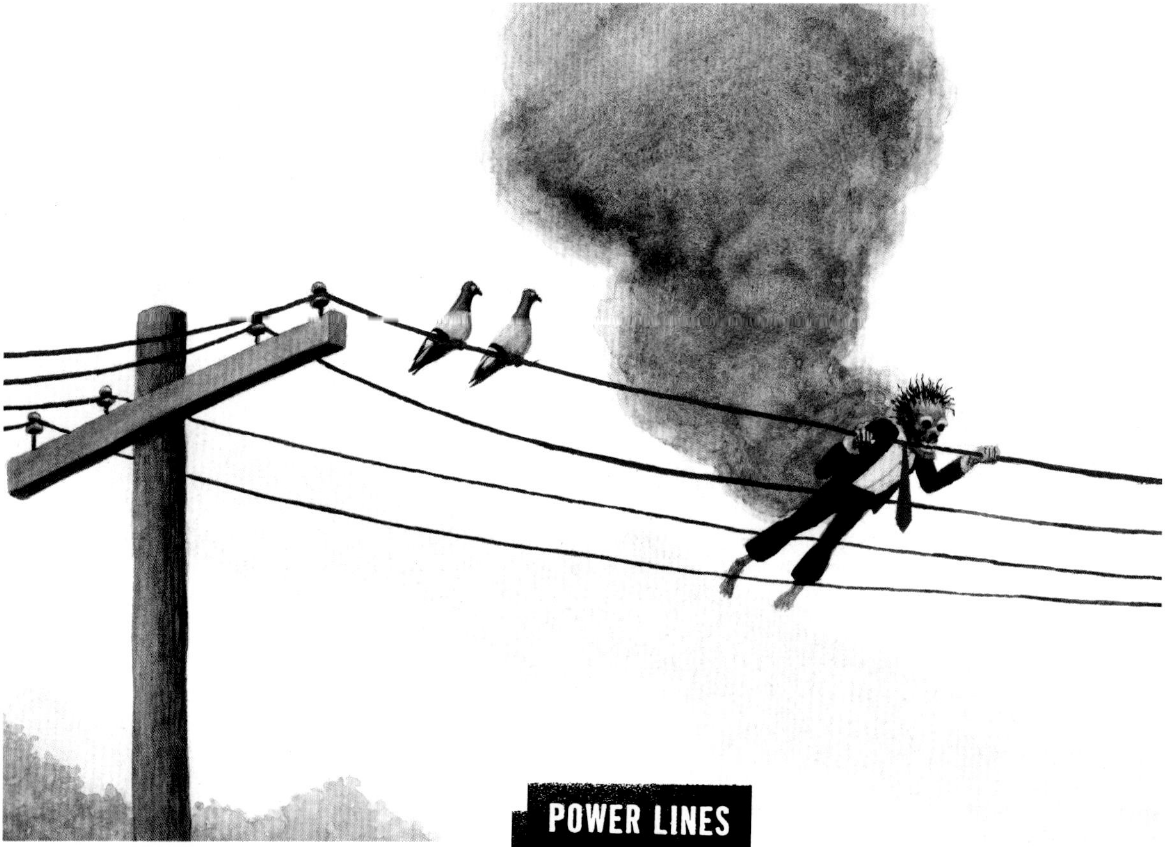

POWER LINES

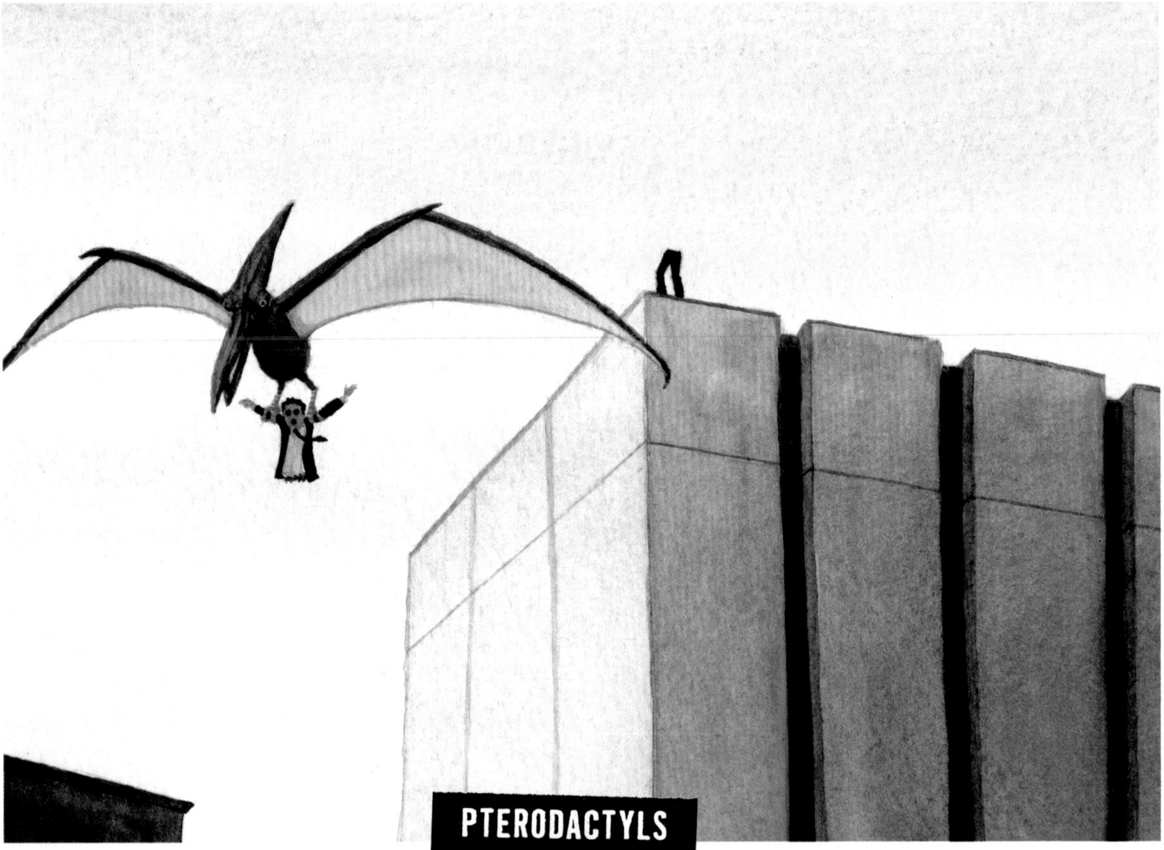

PTERODACTYLS

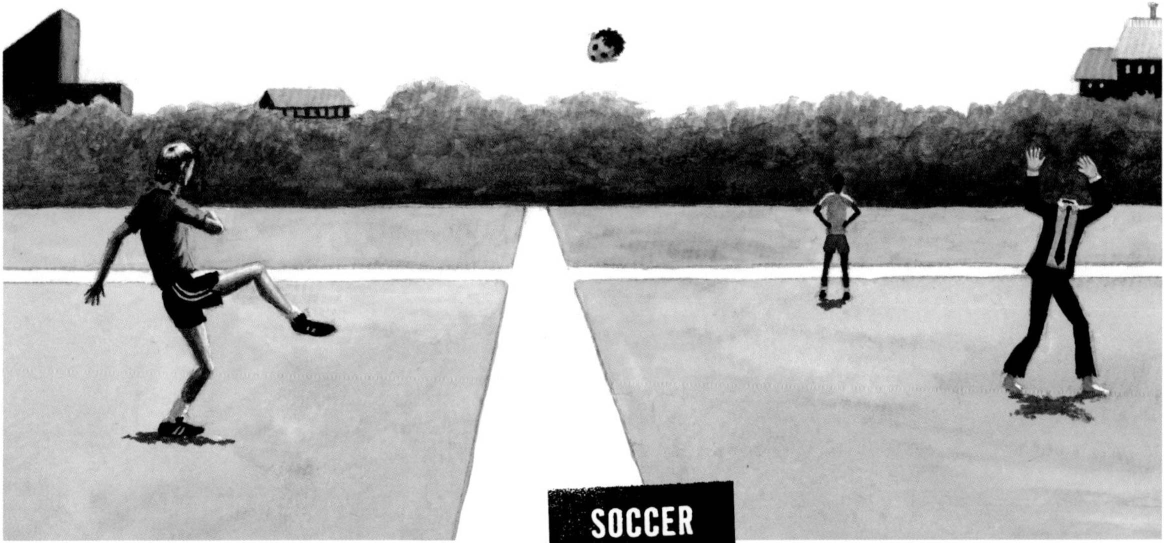

SOCCER

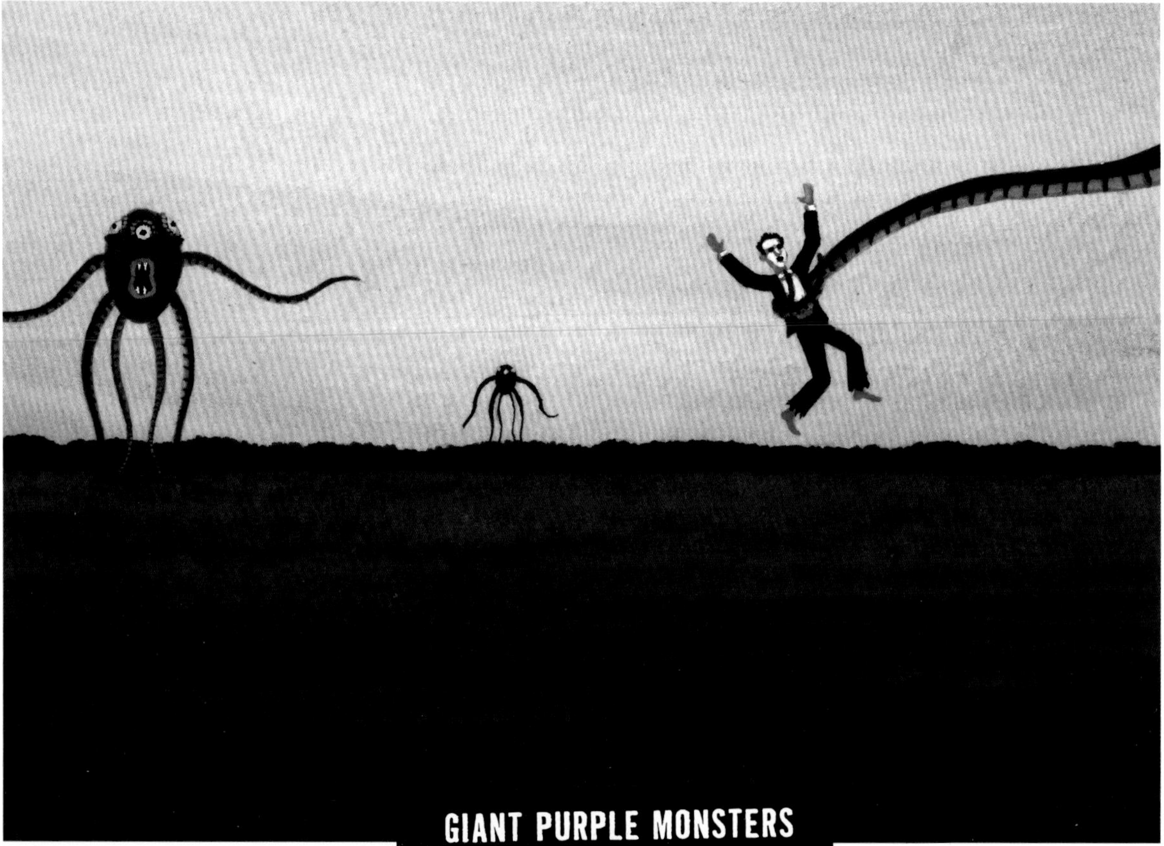

GIANT PURPLE MONSTERS

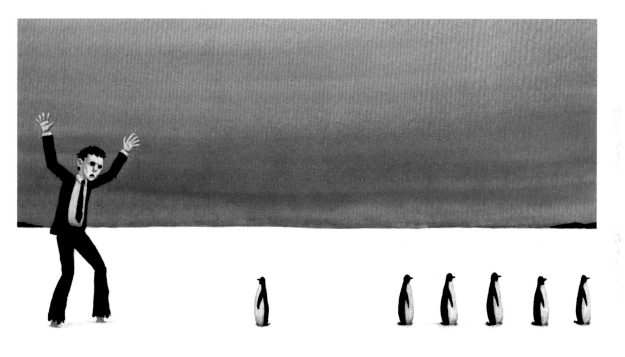

REGULAR PENGUINS

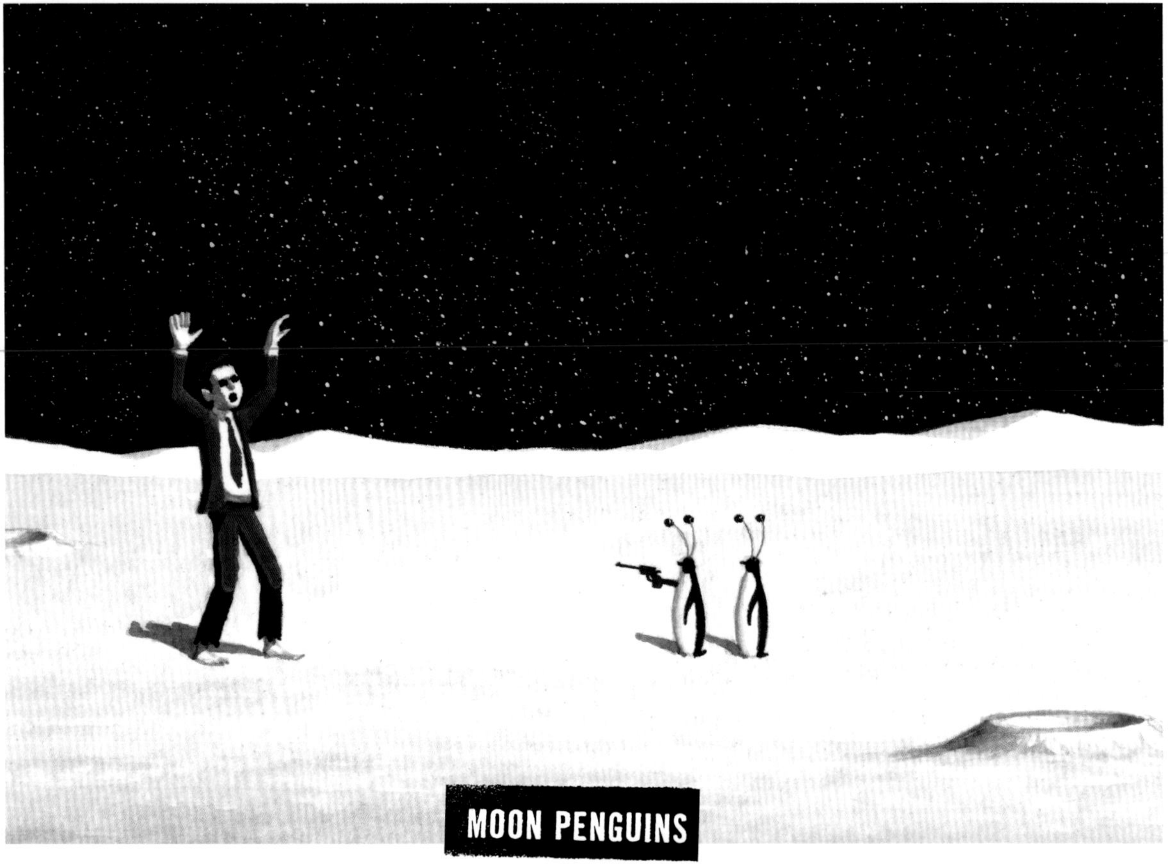
MOON PENGUINS

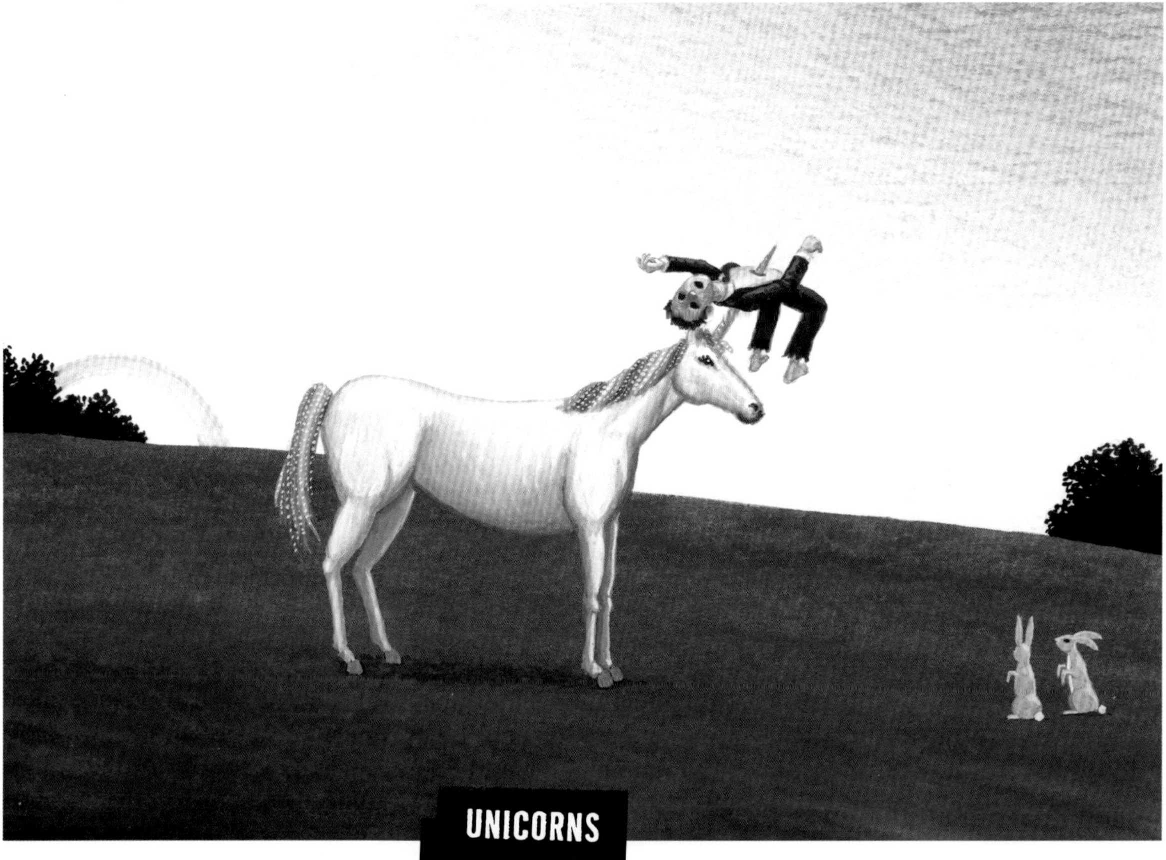

UNICORNS

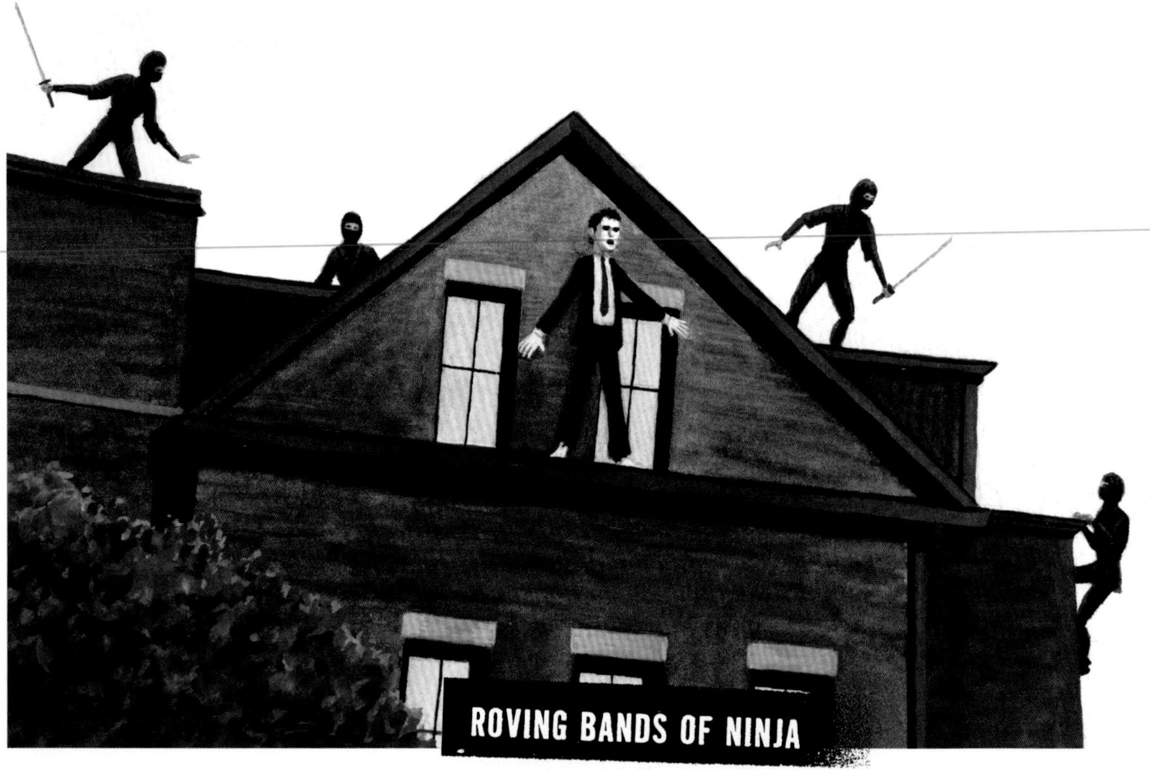

ROVING BANDS OF NINJA

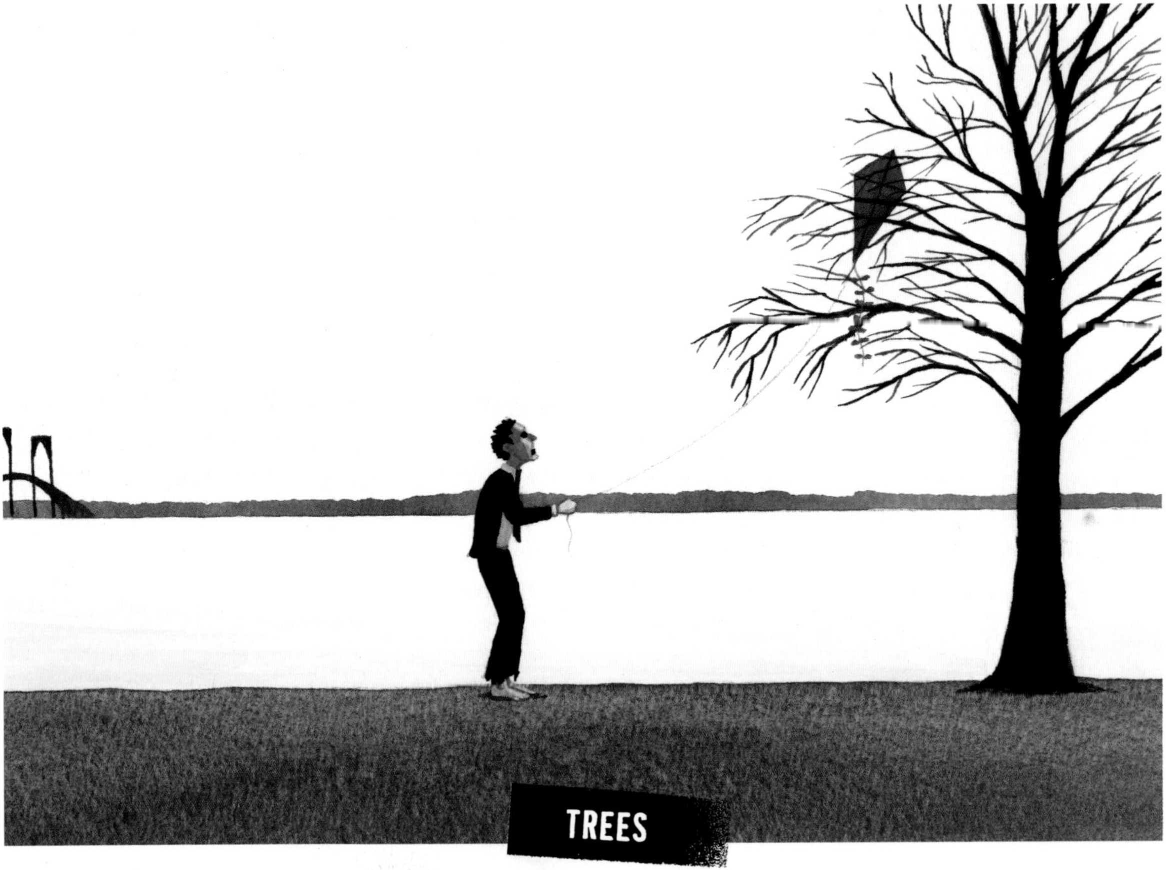
TREES

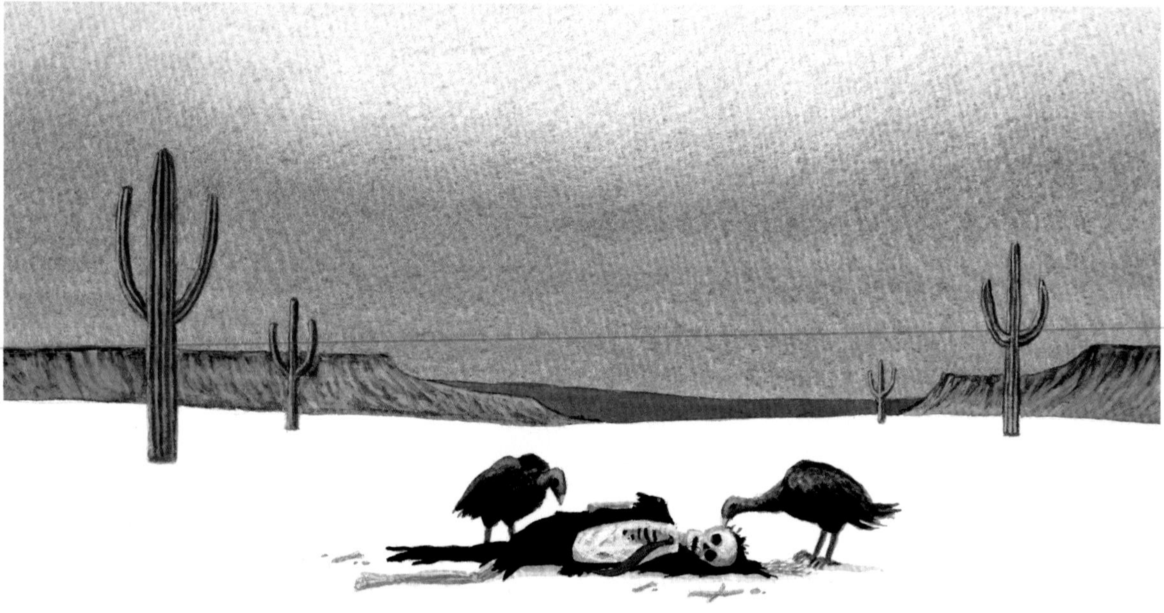

VULTURES

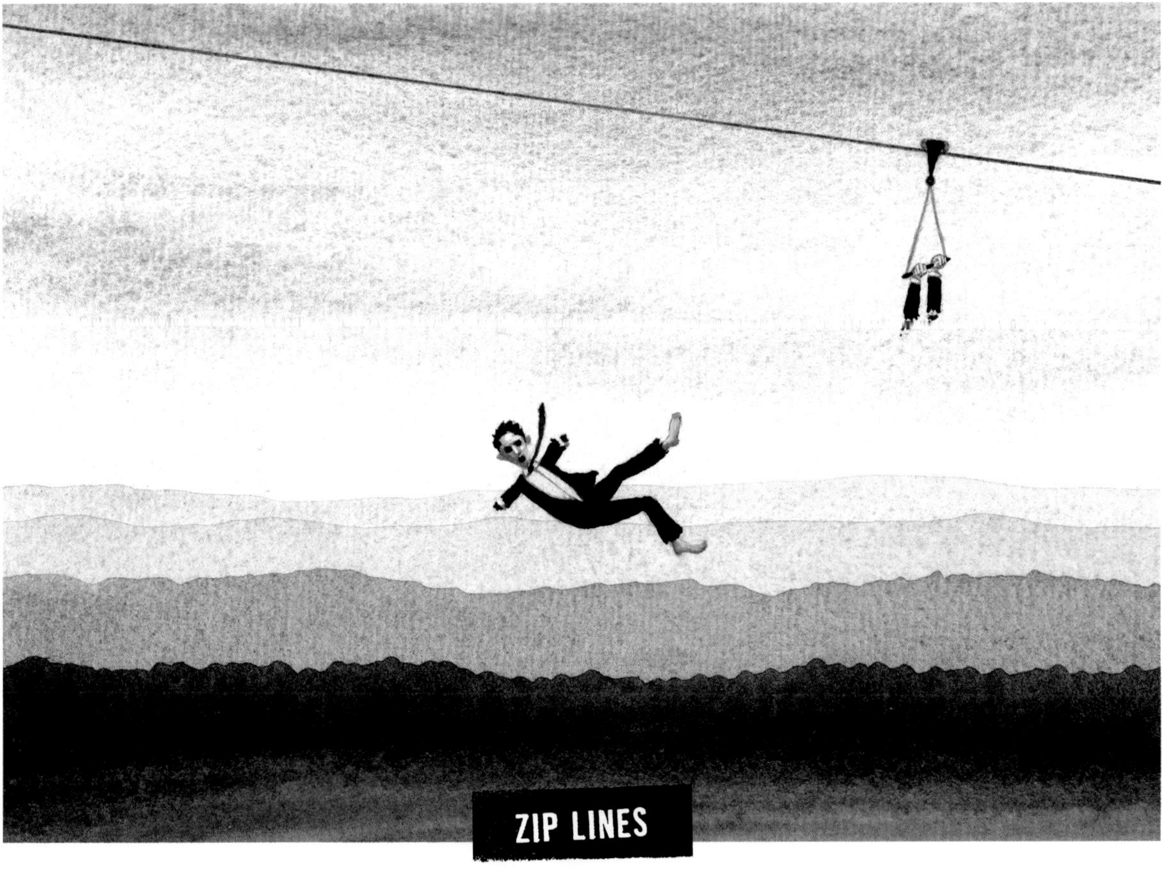
ZIP LINES

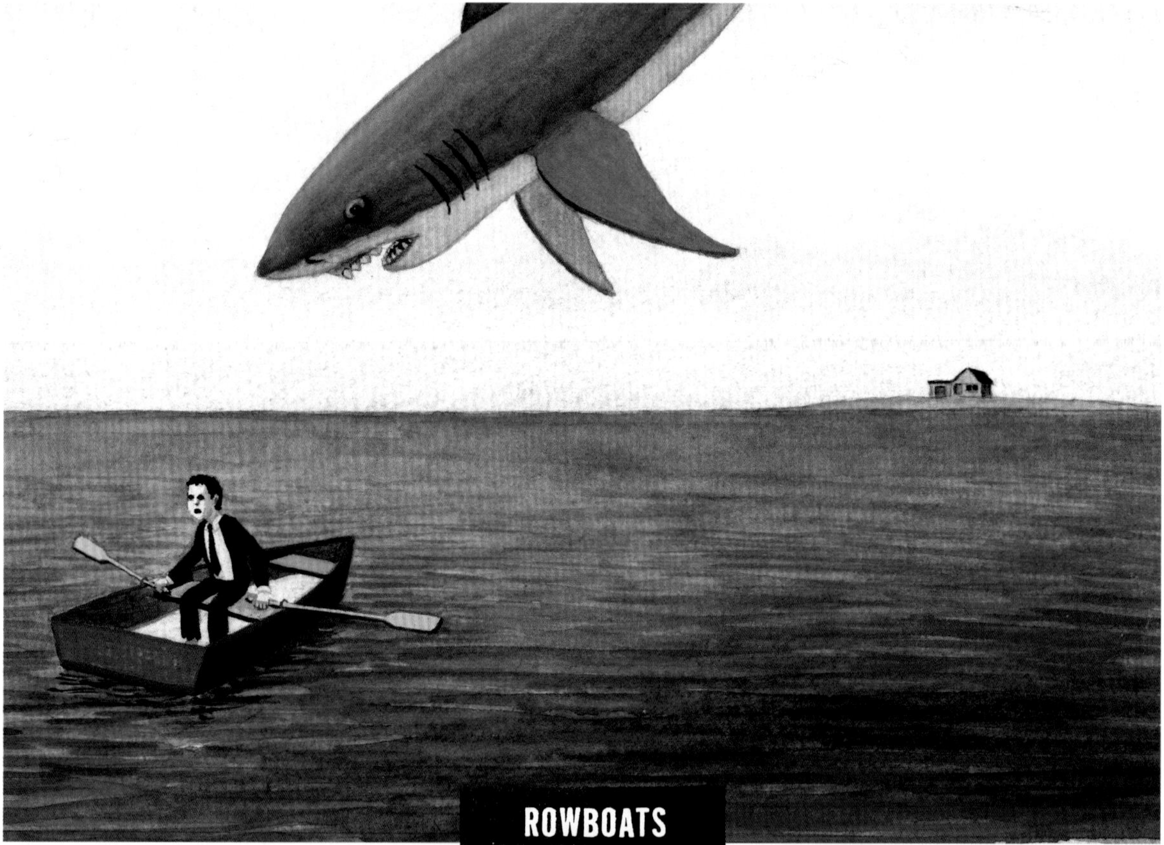

ROWBOATS

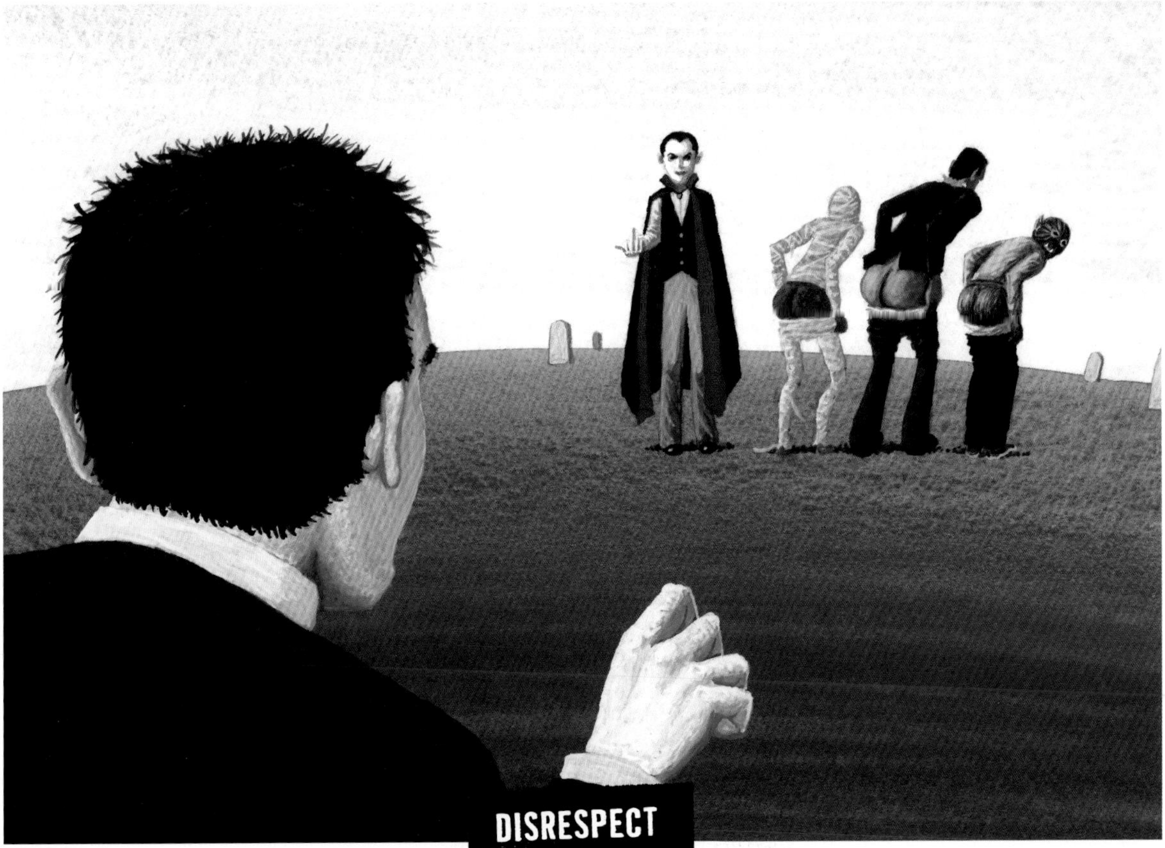

DISRESPECT

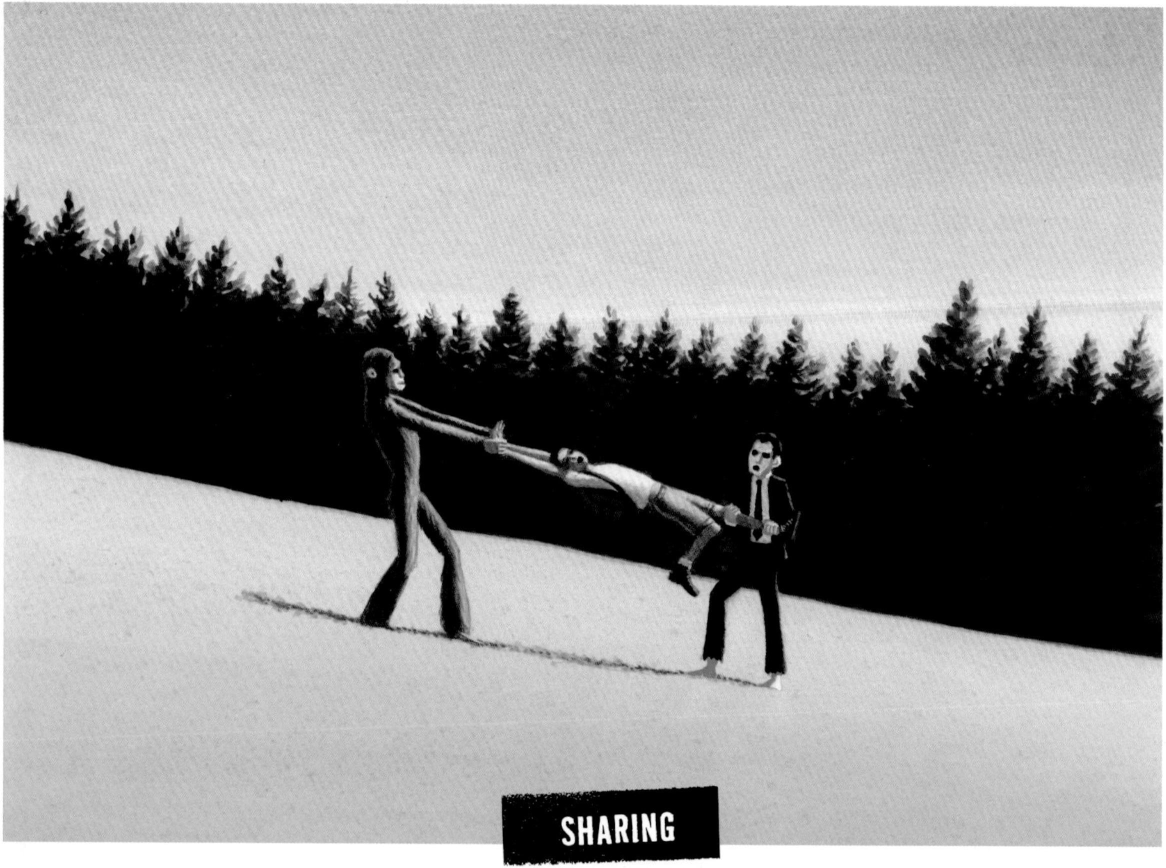

SHARING